CHICAGO CUBS

A Curated History of the North Siders

BRUCE MILES
AND JESSE ROGERS

TRIUMPH
BOOKS

THE FRANCHISE

Library of Congress Cataloging-in-Publication Data

Names: Rogers, Jesse, author. | Miles, Bruce, author.
Title: The franchise Chicago Cubs: a curated history of the North Siders / Jesse Rogers and Bruce Miles.
Other titles: Chicago Cubs
Description: Chicago, Illinois: Triumph Books, [2023] | Includes bibliographical references.
Identifiers: LCCN 2022054857 | ISBN 9781637270028 (cloth)
Subjects: LCSH: Chicago Cubs (Baseball team)—History. | BISAC: SPORTS & RECREATION / Baseball / General | TRAVEL / United States / Midwest / East North Central (IL, IN, MI, OH, WI)
Classification: LCC GV875.C6 R64 2023 | DDC 796.357/640977311—dc23/eng/20221117
LC record available at https://lccn.loc.gov/2022054857

This book is available in quantity at special discounts for your group or organization. For further information, contact:

Triumph Books LLC
814 North Franklin Street
Chicago, Illinois 60610
(312) 337-0747
www.triumphbooks.com

Printed in U.S.A.
ISBN: 978-1-63727-002-8
Design by Preston Pisellini
Page production by NordCompo

To the memory of Neil Peart. RIP, Professor.
"The point of the journey is not to arrive. Anything can happen."

—B.M.

To my kids—Nate, Carly, and Emily.

—J.R.

CONTENTS

PART 4 The Lovable Losers

PART 5 The Oddities

Foreword

REPRESENTING THE CHICAGO CUBS AND WEARING THAT UNIFORM has been life-changing for me. It's put me on a journey that I never thought I would be on. Many—if not all—of the good things that have come my way have come from my teammates, that ballpark, and that fanbase. Being able to come over here, win a World Series, and be a small part of something special is something I'm forever grateful for. That fanbase spans the country, and those fans always treat me and Cubs players so lovingly.

Being part of the Cubs, you feel like you are part of Major League Baseball royalty as one of the staple franchises. You're talking about the Boston Red Sox, the Los Angeles Dodgers, the New York Yankees, and us. No matter where you go, there are Cubs fans. Cubs Nation is truly everywhere. And there's a sense the fans are in it with you. It's a lot of love and support—more than in most places. And now there's an expectation. I think we raised the bar in 2016, and the expectations are higher, but the fanbase is always supportive, loving, and in the fight with you. I can't say that about everywhere I've played. It's a special, special place, and the fanbase is what really makes it unique along with the historic ballpark.

It starts with playing at Wrigley Field, and that schedule, which is unlike any other team's. No one else in baseball can relate to it with so many day games throughout the year. You can look at that in two different ways. You can think about it being a positive or negative, but I always thought from a player's standpoint, it was great. I got to have breakfast with my kids and go to work a little bit like a normal job. On Friday night I could have dinner with my family, go to a show or a movie, and go home and have that normal life we all want.

Playing and living in that neighborhood is one of my favorite parts of Wrigley. On a nice summer night, you can just either ride your bike or walk to the ballpark. I remember 2015 and 2016 so vividly when I'd walk to the ballpark down Southport, and fans would line up to wish me good luck that day. Everyone was so supportive as I walked to work. I'd often get asked: "Can I grab a picture with you, Rossy?"

I've got two favorite Wrigley moments. One is selfish. My last home game was on ESPN's *Sunday Night Baseball*. I hit a home run against the St. Louis Cardinals. I got two standing ovations. It was my last regular-season game. Manager Joe Maddon ended up taking me out, and I got another standing ovation. That was great. The other one that stands out to me is Miguel Montero's grand slam against the Dodgers in the National League Championship Series in 2016. That place was shaking, man. I'm sure during Kerry Wood's 20-strikeout game and in other big moments covered in this book it was the same way, but for me Montero's home run was as special as any moment I've been a part of.

And then there's the history of it all, which this book captures through the personalities of its players and managers. If you watch all the highlights over the years, you realize it's all in the same space. There's an aura to it. The best players in and out of a Cubs uniform stepped foot on this field. Memories build up. For example, every time a right fielder runs out to his position, I get images of Sammy Sosa running out there. I'm sure there are images like that for fans every time they step into the stadium. I think that's where the love from fans comes from. It's a special ballpark where everyone wants to come experience a great show and a great product and make a memory. I'm so happy that I've been able to be a part of it and still be a part of it.

So when I think about putting on that Cubs uniform, I think about the atmosphere around Wrigley. Wearing those pinstripes on a beautiful summer afternoon in Chicago and seeing fans with a beer in their hand excited for each and every game is what summer is supposed to be. And the Wrigleyville neighborhood has that energy and buzz to it. There's nothing like it.

And there's no one better to tell so many of the interesting stories involving this storied franchise than longtime scribes Jesse Rogers and Bruce Miles. Enjoy!

—*David Ross*

PART 1

THE STARS

1

Gabby Hartnett and His Homer in the Gloamin'

MOST LONGTIME BASEBALL FANS CAN QUICKLY RATTLE OFF the most memorable walk-off home runs in big league history. Bobby Thomson's "Shot Heard 'Round the World" at the Polo Grounds gave the New York Giants a victory against the Brooklyn Dodgers to clinch the 1951 National League pennant in a three-game playoff. The home run is immortalized by Giants radio announcer Russ Hodges bellowing, "The Giants win the pennant! The Giants win the pennant! The Giants win the pennant!"

Bill Mazeroski's drive over the left-field wall at Forbes Field gave the Pittsburgh Pirates a Game Seven victory against

THE FRANCHISE: CHICAGO CUBS

the New York Yankees in the 1960 World Series. Joe Carter's line drive against Mitch Williams of the Philadelphia Phillies at SkyDome gave the Toronto Blue Jays their second straight World Series title in 1993. Carlton Fisk's shot off the left-field foul pole at Fenway Park won Game Six of the 1975 World Series against the Cincinnati Reds to send the Fall Classic to a Game Seven. Fisk's willing the ball fair remains immortalized thanks to a cameraman inside of Fenway's Green Monster.

Ozzie Smith's unlikely homer in Game Five of the 1985 National League Championship Series against the Los Angeles Dodgers at Busch Stadium in St. Louis moved Cardinals announcer Jack Buck to tell Redbirds fans to: "Go crazy, folks, go crazy!" Also involving the Dodgers: a hobbling Kirk Gibson's unlikely homer off Dennis Eckersley in Game One of the 1988 World Series propelled the Los Angeles Dodgers to a sweep of the favored Oakland A's.

The list goes on and includes Kirby Puckett's homer in Game Six of the 1991 World Series to send the Minnesota Twins to a Game Seven against the Cardinals, a series the Twins won the next night. David Ortiz's homer at Fenway Park in Game Four of the 2004 American League Championship Series kept the Red Sox from being swept and sparked an improbable comeback that sent the Red Sox all the way to a world championship, their first since 1918.

But one dramatic and important walk-off homer, which involved the Chicago Cubs, has been lost in the fog of time and history. In fact, you won't even find it in the Top 50 walk-off homers compiled in 2011 by Bleacher Report.

That homer happened as darkness was setting in at Wrigley Field on the late afternoon of September 28, 1938. Actually, it wasn't the fog; it was the gloaming or the "gloamin'" as it was coined by Earl Hilligan of the Associated Press. The "Homer in the Gloamin'" was hit by Hall of Fame catcher Gabby Hartnett, breaking a 5–5 tie with the Pirates and putting the Cubs into the driver's seat for the 1938 National League pennant, which they clinched three days later.

Had Hartnett not homered and the Cubs not scored in the bottom of the ninth inning, the game would have been called on account of darkness and, under the rules of the day, it would have to be replayed in its entirety, perhaps changing the course of the title chase's final outcome.

That Hartnett's homer has been largely forgotten is both a shame and a mystery. After all, ol' Gabby is one of the biggest names and most important players in Cubs history. He was behind the plate six years earlier at Wrigley Field, where Babe Ruth allegedly called his shot in the 1932 World Series. (Ruth most likely didn't call it.) Despite it happening so long ago, that has become an ingrained part of baseball history and folklore.

But what of Hartnett and his homer?

One can easily imagine that home run being hit today and the subsequent madness on social media—not to mention it being replayed endless times on *SportsCenter* and TV outlets in Chicago and across the nation. "There's no footage of it," said research historian Ed Hartig. "There's very few pictures of it. What if there were social media? When [quarterback Justin] Fields of the Bears hit a home run [in batting practice], there's like five different angles of it. Gabby Hartnett, there's the one picture behind home plate where you see the Andy Frain usher behind him. Then there's another photo where the field is being kind of overrun. But that's it.

"The Cubs were seven games out. They were in fourth place with a month to go. If I had to pick four events I'd want to go to at Wrigley Field before the 2016 postseason, I said Kerry Wood's 20-strikeout game, Gale Sayers' six-touchdown game, the ski-jumping event in '42, and Hartnett's Homer in the Gloamin.' It's one of the four greatest events at Wrigley Field. I think it's one of the four most important moments at the ballpark."

But alas, there was no social media in 1938 (perhaps a blessing to those souls alive then). And the game was broadcast only on radio. Unless someone emerges with it, there is no film record of Hartnett's Homer in the Gloamin'. There are only black-and-white images taken by photographers on the scene that September day.

So who was Gabby Hartnett and how good was he? Charles Leo Hartnett was born in Woonsocket, Rhode Island, at the dawn of the 20th century on December 20, 1900. According to an article by Bill Johnson for sabr.org (the Society for American Baseball Research), Hartnett was given the ironic nickname "Gabby" early in his Cubs career because of his shy reticence. Hartnett said he was following his mother's advice to be seen and not heard when he first joined the Cubs. Later, Hartnett would become one of the more friendly players and a garrulous presence behind the plate, the Most Voluble Player, if you will.

The 1935 National League MVP, Hartnett played for the Cubs from 1922 to 1940 before ending his playing career with the New York Giants in 1941. A check of the Cubs' leader boards reveals that Hartnett ranks in the franchise's top 10 in: games played (1,926), home runs (231), doubles (391), total bases (3,079), RBIs (1,153), extra-base hits (686), wins above replacement (55), defensive wins above replacement (13.3), and runs created (1,129).

Hartnett was so good that the *Chicago Tribune*'s Jerome Holtzman, the "Dean of Chicago baseball writers," named Hartnett as the best player in Cubs history in 1989 ahead of even

Ernie Banks. (Sammy Sosa didn't join the Cubs until 1992.) "If baseball was strictly a home run contest, there is absolutely no question about the best all-time Cub player," Holtzman wrote. "It would be Ernie Banks. But the assignment is to list, in order, the 10 best all-round players, not the best home-run hitter, nor the best defensive player, nor the best base runner. And Leo 'Gabby' Hartnett, in my opinion, was the best all-around player. Like Banks, he played with the Cubs for 19 years, from 1922–40. Unlike Banks, who was never on a winner, Hartnett was with four championship Cub teams—1929, '32, '35, and '38. He sat out almost the entire '29 season with an injured arm. But he was the pivotal player on the three other pennant clubs."

Holtzman sought to buttress his opinion with testimonials from others who were with the Cubs. "Jim Gallagher, the one-time Cubs general manager, offered what I regard as the best summation: 'Banks was a great ballplayer,' Gallagher said. 'But Gabby was a great, great ballplayer. For winning, I would have to take Gabby.'"

There were more testimonials. "He was the best player on our club all the time I was there," insisted Billy Herman, the Cubs' Hall of Fame second baseman. "Sure, we had some pretty good ballplayers. But there was no way we could have won without him."

Holtzman acknowledged that such player accounts could be suspect. And he also cited "intangibles" in making his case for Hartnett being the greatest Cub. "But statistics alone cannot convey Hartnett's principal value, his leadership on the field. He was constantly talking it up, encouraging, exhorting, sometimes admonishing his teammates to greater effort," Holtzman wrote. "When the club was faltering, he was appointed player/manager. This was in July 1938. Two months later, on September 28, against the league-leading Pittsburgh Pirates at Wrigley Field,

Hartnett, at 37, came through with the biggest clutch hit in Cub history: his legendary 'Homer in the Gloamin'."

Hartnett also was involved in some of the biggest moments in baseball before he smacked the "Homer in the Gloamin'." He was behind the plate when Ruth allegedly called his shot in Game Three of the 1932 World Series against Cubs pitcher Charlie Root, who steadfastly maintained that Ruth never called his shot despite Ruth fueling the myth. Hartnett agreed with his pitcher. "I don't want to take anything from the Babe because he's the reason we made good money, but he didn't call the shot," Hartnett told his biographer. "He held up the index finger of his left hand...and said, 'It only takes one to hit.'"

Hartnett was the catcher during the 1934 All-Star Game, where New York Giants pitcher Carl Hubbell struck out in succession Hall of Famers Ruth, Lou Gehrig, Jimmie Foxx, Al Simmons, and Joe Cronin. In the 1937 All-Star Game, Hartnett was the catcher when Dizzy Dean was hit on the toe by a line drive. The injury forced Dean to alter his delivery, effectively leading to the premature end of him being an elite pitcher.

In 1938 the Cubs capped a run, in which they won pennants every three years: 1929, 1932, 1935, and 1938. Managing the Cubs to National League championships in '32 and '35 was Charlie Grimm, who doubled as a player/manager in those two seasons. Known as "Jolly Cholly," Grimm was a popular figure in Chicago known for his left-handed banjo playing in addition to his baseball playing. Grimm eventually would serve three terms as manager of the Cubs with his last coming in 1960.

The 1938 season began well enough, if not spectacularly, for the Cubs. They went into first place with a 27–16 record on June 5 before winning their next two games. The team fell into a funk after that was capped by a six-game losing streak from July 4–12. Rumors began swirling in the Chicago newspapers that Grimm was on the hot seat. The Cubs rallied with a seven-game winning streak after the losing skid, but the chemistry seemed off.

Owner P.K. Wrigley summoned newspaper beat writers to his office on July 20, an off day caused by a scheduled double-header with the Brooklyn Dodgers being rained out. There, he announced that he was firing Grimm and naming Hartnett player/manager. Both Grimm and Hartnett entered the office after Wrigley made his announcement. The team was 45–36 at the time, five-and-a-half games behind the Pirates. "Grimm has done a swell job, but the club has not done as well as we felt it should," Wrigley said.

Jolly Cholly took the news without apparent bitterness, and Hartnett accepted the challenge. "Well, this is a surprise," Gabby told the *Tribune*. "Naturally, I will do what I can to win pennant."

Spirits improved, but the Cubs found themselves nine games behind the Pirates on August 20 after a stretch of six losses in seven games. But the team went on a tear, pulling to within two-and-a-half games of the lead on September 14. The Cubs had won eight in a row and were within a half game on September 28 after Dean beat the Pirates 2–1 the previous day before 42,238 in a Wrigley Field thriller that took just one hour and 38 minutes to play.

The fateful game of September 28 began with a pitching matchup of the Pirates' Bob Klinger against Clay Bryant of the Cubs, who took a 1–0 lead in the second inning. Then the Pirates went ahead 3–1 in the sixth before the Cubs quickly tied the game in the bottom of the inning. Each team scored twice in the eighth to make it 5–5.

Games in those days began at 3:00 PM, and with darkness beginning to descend on Wrigley Field (which did not get lights for another 50 years), umpires decided that the ninth inning would be the final inning. If the game remained tied, it would be replayed the following day.

Of all people, Root took the mound for the Cubs to face the top of the Pittsburgh order. Root allowed only a single in a scoreless frame, leaving the Cubs to face Mace Brown, one of the baseball's early relief specialists in the 1930s. Cubs legend Phil Cavarretta began the bottom of the ninth with a fly-out to center before Carl Reynolds grounded out to second base.

Up stepped Hartnett. Brown quickly got ahead in the count 0–2 on a pair of curveballs. Brown tried to sneak another curve past Hartnett, but he later recounted that he made a bad pitch, one that landed into the left-field bleachers to give the Cubs a dramatic 6–5 victory and vault them into first place. The scene that followed was chaotic as Hartnett rounded the bases in the gloaming and had plenty of company. "The mob started to gather around Gabby before he had reached first base," went the account in the *Chicago Tribune*. "By the time he had rounded second, he couldn't have been recognized in the mass of Cub players, frenzied fans, and excited ushers but for that red face that shone out, even in the gray shadows. After the skipper finally had struggled to the plate, things became worse. The ushers, who had fanned out to form a protective barrier around the infield, forgot their constantly rehearsed pretty maneuver and rushed to save Hartnett's life. They tugged and they shoved and finally they started swinging their fists before the players could carry their boss into the safety afforded by the tunnel behind the Cub dugout.

"There was a new hysteria after Gabby reached the catwalk, which leads to the clubhouse. But by the time the gendarmes were organized, Gabby got to the bathhouse without being stripped by souvenir maniacs."

Brown, who lived to almost 93 years old, told writer George Wine: "Gabby must have swung at what he heard because it was too dark for him to see the ball."

Legendary sports columnist John Carmichael, whose "Barber Shop" column would become a staple in the *Chicago Daily News*, tried to come to grips with what he saw on that September day-turned-gloaming in 1938. "We surrender to inadequacy," Carmichael wrote. "This Cub–Pirate pennant fight has gone beyond our poor power to picture in words. So let this be, today, a confession of helplessness to treat an afternoon that beggars description, an afternoon in the life of a stout hearted Irishman who, as darkness almost wrapped him from the sight of 35,000 quaking fans, changed the map of the baseball world with one devastating blow."

Next to Ruth's called shot six years earlier, Hartnett's "Homer in the Gloamin'" (as it was christened by a wire-service writer) may have been the biggest home run in the history of baseball at the time. Just as the homer has largely been forgotten, the word "gloaming" is another you don't hear anymore. It's derived from old English and was popular in Scots usage.

The "Homer in the Gloamin'" moniker was a play on the song, "Roamin' in the Gloamin'" written by Harry Lauder in 1911. You can see the Scots influence in the lyrics:

"Roamin' in the gloamin' on the bonnie banks o' Clyde.
Roamin' in the gloamin' wae my lassie by my sideband.
When the sun has gone to rest,
That's the time we love the best."

The Cubs in 1938 drew 951,640 fans to Wrigley Field. In the latter years of the Great Depression, this led all National League teams in attendance. The hysteria of the day faded as time went on—the Cubs were swept in the World Series by the vaunted New York Yankees and didn't return to the Fall Classic until 1945, when they lost to the Detroit Tigers.

Hartnett wound up settling in the Chicago area, where he ran a bowling alley. He died on his birthday in 1972. His 231 homers with the Cubs place him eighth on the team's all-time list—he was first on the list until being passed by Banks in 1960. Players such as Billy Williams and Sosa came along and also passed Hartnett in homers. Banks' 500th homer in 1970 and the homers Sosa hit during his 1998 assault on Roger Maris' single-season record (in his duel with the Cardinals' Mark McGwire) are ingrained in the minds of latter-day Cubs fans as are walk-off homers by Willie Smith in the 1969 Wrigley Field opener and Williams' game-ending homer off Bob Gibson on Opening Day in 1971.

Hartnett's homer has been lost in, well, the gloamin', even though he is immortalized in Cooperstown and is a member of the Cubs Hall of Fame, which opened in 2021. Even today, for those who do acknowledge the importance of Hartnett's historic blast, many think it clinched the pennant. "When you do hear the story, you hear stuff like, 'Oh, it won the pennant.' It didn't win the pennant," Hartig said. "But all summer they're chasing the Pirates and they finally catch them. This is Chicago. This isn't Minnesota. This is Chicago! There's no TV. There's few pictures. It's just been kind of forgotten. There's no evidence of it other than, 'There it is in the newspaper.' How do you immortalize it at a ballpark? There's a Hartnett flag on the roof. Hartnett's got a plaque in the Hall of Fame. They're not going to do a statue of him. The guys who got statues is not only because they're top of the leaderboard, but 20 to 30 years after they were done playing, they were still around. Gabby Hartnett ran his bowling alley. He kind of disappeared. He lived in Des

Plaines. He occasionally came back for a Hall of Fame type of thing, but he kind of stayed away. So you're not going to see a statue of Hartnett. If they did, I wouldn't complain."

* * *

Whenever Joanne Biebrach attends a Chicago Cubs game, she proudly wears a Cubs jersey with "HARTNETT 9" on the back. Biebrach is a granddaughter of Gabby Hartnett. She was nine years old when her grandfather died, but she does have memories. "He enjoyed playing with us and everything like that," she said. "He was a family man. He was a good guy. I remember him sitting in his easy chair watching a baseball game, having a radio over here listening to another game and having another transistor over here with one in his ear and listening to that one. I don't know how he did it, but he would pay attention to all three ballgames at once. I know he had the bowling alley. Everybody talks about the bowling alley. I remember seeing him there. It had a shooting gallery in the basement. He was a jolly fun old guy as I remember it."

The "HARTNETT 9" jersey no doubt is an eyecatcher, as are other old-time jerseys people wear to the ballpark. Although it doesn't happen as often as it used to, people sometimes stop Biebrach when they see her in the jersey. "I do get reactions from people there," she said. "My husband is really great whenever somebody brings up baseball. He makes sure that person knows that I'm a descendant. It's fun. What I like, and it doesn't happen as much anymore, when we'd get an old-timer and they would find out I'm Gabby Hartnett's granddaughter, they would always have a story. One guy, I remember, told me he was a little kid, and they were going to have the Cubs come out to his baseball field and play catch with them. He got up that day, and he and his friends were all ready for it, and it was pouring rain. They were thinking, 'Well, they're not going to show up.' They went to the field anyway because they're young kids. They got their mitts. The rains stops, and lo and behold, Gabby shows up. He plays ball with them for like an hour and talks to them. The man said, 'It was the best day of my life.' Stuff like that, when people tell me that, it just gets to me."

Hartnett was so accommodating that he gave an autograph to a child with Al Capone during a 1931 charity game between the Cubs and Chicago White Sox at Comiskey Park. "He would never turn down a kid who asked for an autograph or anything like that," Biebrach said. "Hence, the picture of him with Al Capone, that famous picture. He just went up because the kid asked for an autograph. He didn't know Al Capone was there. Then someone said, 'Gabby, don't do that.' Gabby said, 'Yeah, you tell him he can't have the autograph.'"

According to several reports, including one from the New England Historical Society, it was none other than commissioner Kenesaw Mountain Landis who was anything but thrilled with Hartnett accommodating the child with Capone. A decade earlier, Landis permanently banned eight members of the White Sox, dubbed the "Black Sox," from baseball for consorting with gamblers to throw the 1919 World Series against the Cincinnati Reds. "Commissioner Kenesaw Mountain Landis was furious," according to the New England Historical Society's website. "There are several versions of the story. In one, Landis sent him a telegram that said, 'You are no longer allowed to have your picture taken with Al Capone.' Hartnett sent him a telegram saying, 'Okay, but if you don't want me having my picture taken with Al Capone, you tell him.' According to another version, Landis chastised him personally. Gabby Hartnett replied: 'I go to his place of business, why shouldn't he come to mine?'"

As far as the "Homer in the Gloamin'" being lost to time, Biebrach simply says that: "People forget. Time makes you forget."

In addition to memories, Biebrach has opinions. One of those, agreed with by many and backed up by the numbers, is that Hartnett is the greatest Cubs catcher of all time. His 55 WAR with the Cubs puts him well ahead of fellow Cubs catchers Johnny Kling, Willson Contreras, Jody Davis, and Randy Hundley.

Biebrach beams with pride when she talks about her grandfather, both as baseball player and as a man. "Definitely, that home run in the gloaming, it was huge thing," she said. "I do believe that he was the greatest catcher the Cubs have had. I don't think they've had a better one. His whole life was baseball when he was playing it. He still holds a few records still at Wrigley. Every time I go there, sometimes I see something on their pregame thing. He's usually there. There's bricks for him and there are banners for him. I think that his number should be retired. Know that he would show up in the rain to play catch with kids when he could have easily said, 'No, it's not going to happen because it's raining.' He would be the guy to show up. He was that guy."

2

Andre Dawson

It was the winter of 1986, and the Chicago Cubs weren't necessarily searching for a new right fielder—at least not until one dropped into their laps. Andre Nolan Dawson—known as the "Hawk"—was in the middle of a fine career with the Montreal Expos. He was drafted by them in 1975 and almost immediately made it to the big leagues. Dawson spent his formative years in Montreal—well before they moved to Washington, D.C., and became known as the Nationals.

From 1976 to 1986, he made a name for himself, winning Rookie of the Year in 1977 and then leading the league in hits in 1983. He was an imposing presence at the plate, as evidenced by him also leading the league in getting hit by a pitch four different times in a six-year span.

Dawson could play longball or small ball. One year he had 18 sacrifice flies and another year had eight sacrifice bunts. But it was his power and strong arm, which became a staple across the National League. At a time when hitting 20 home runs in a season held meaning, Dawson hit at least that many seven times in a nine-year span, but playing on the artificial surface at Olympic Stadium took its toll on his knees. That would actually benefit the Cubs in the weeks and months to come.

After yet another 20-home run campaign, Dawson was in need of a new contract in Montreal. What ensued in the following months between the end of the 1986 season and the beginning of 1987 would be one of the most unique stories a player has ever experienced. Adding even more drama would be what happened between April and October in 1987 as Dawson's career as a Cub took off.

But first he had to become a Cub.

The Expos finished the 1986 season in fourth place with a 78–83 record. There was little drama to the end of their season. That would come soon after.

Dawson was coming off a good year but not one of his very best. He had compiled an OPS-plus of 123—better than his previous two seasons but not a career high. He was making about $1.2 million and in his mind was due for a raise. "At the meeting with the Expos—the owner in particular—the last day of the season, they made an offer," Dawson explained. "They made an offer to me, which called for a cut in pay as a free agent pending."

The multiple Gold Glove winner and All-Star couldn't believe what he was hearing. At first, he figured it was a preliminary meeting but still had reservations. "I didn't have a good feeling about them making me an offer, which called for a cut in pay, after being there for 10 years," Dawson said. "And that was with me having some leverage going forward as an agent. So we didn't really get anywhere with the owner."

The Expos wanted to cut Dawson's pay by about $200,000. As the offseason progressed, Montreal refused to budge. "I remember making the comment to the team president, John McHale, that it wasn't going to work," Dawson said. "'And I just appreciate the fact that you gave me the first 10 years my career.' They gave me the opportunity, but I was prepared to go ahead and move forward and I was going to test the free-agent market. And that's pretty much how things went the rest of the winter. There was no contact from any of the teams. I saw the end of February then March roll around, and still there was no contact."

What Dawson didn't know at the time was that team owners weren't exactly acting in good faith during those years in the '80s. Later, they would be accused and found guilty of collusion. As part of the owners' and players' collective bargaining agreement—a document which spells out the rules of the game on and off the field—there's a clause which states "clubs shall not act in concert with other clubs." In this case, however, collusion led to owners suppressing salaries. In practice it was pretty simple: teams agreed not to drive up the price of players by bidding on them. Instead, they held the line and simply didn't offer them market value. Where else could players go to make a living playing baseball? It was illegal and would eventually cost the owners millions in damages. Dawson would be a casualty that winter but one which eventually benefited the Cubs.

By this time in 1987, spring training had started, and Dawson needed a new strategy because he was still without a job. He met with his agent, Dick Moss, in California to come up with a gameplan. Waiting for teams to come to him just wasn't happening. "We came to the conclusion that we can't really sit down and negotiate a dollar figure or a fair market value with anyone because it just wasn't going to happen," Dawson said.

"So we decided, 'Okay, let's just go to spring training some-where.' And my preference of choice was with the Cubs because they were still in the National League and played on grass."

After deciding his time in Montreal was done, one thing Dawson was certain of was that he no longer wanted to play his home games on the artificial turf. In those days, playing on turf nearly felt like cement. Advancements in artificial surfaces would come much later and long after Dawson was finished with his career. Half of his games every year to that point were played on the hard surface of Olympic Stadium in Montreal. Wrigley Field would offer something different and much better on his knees. Staying in the National League was important because back then teams only played teams in the same league. Dawson didn't want to have to learn all the pitchers in the American League. He just spent a decade mastering the ones in the NL.

There would be yet another aspect working in the Cubs favor. "I'd always had better numbers playing daytime baseball," Dawson said.

Though Wrigley Field would add lights in 1988, the team still played the majority of its games during the day. So nat-ural grass in the National League and playing matinee games led Dawson to the Cubs' spring facility in Mesa, Arizona, that March. "The other choice was Atlanta because it was again in the National League and on a natural playing surface," Dawson said. "And it was closer to my home in Florida. So we decided that we would just go unannounced and try and make sure that we could establish some sort of sit down and hear us out, per se."

He just showed up. This was unprecedented, especially for a caliber of player like Dawson. Established major leaguers just don't show up at spring camp without a contract. "Dallas Green, the general manager at the time, wasn't aware that we were there," Dawson said. "We were standing outside the training facility, waiting for the start of practice. And once he was alerted that we were there, we asked if we could come in and meet with him, which he eventually he obliged."

Dawson's appearance at camp on March 2, 1987, created a buzz within the clubhouse and on the practice fields. No one was really sure what to make of it. "I just remembered being out on the field and then him kind of touring around a little bit and walking behind the batting cage," 1984 MVP Ryne Sandberg recalled. "There was some rumblings of this happening, of him showing up. I was happy to see him and I thought that he'd be a tremendous addition to the club. But, yeah, it was kind of a strange thing."

Cubs pitchers, like Greg Maddux and Rick Sutcliffe, were ecstatic at the prospect of signing Dawson. The multi-tool player could come in handy both at the plate and in the out-field. "I knew how special he was," Sutcliffe said. "He produced runs and he took away runs defensively. He could beat you in a lot of different ways with his arm, his bat, his legs. He was just a complete guy."

Maddux added: "The first memory was what he did to get to Chicago. That took a lot of freaking courage to do what he did. I don't think many players would've done that."

In fact, no one could remember a player *ever* just showing up. Sutcliffe was so committed to having Dawson that he offered part of his salary to get him. "I just remember spring training," Sutcliffe said. "Reporters were asking me about Dawson, and I said, 'You know what? Let me start the bidding. I'll give a $100,000 of my own money if we sign him.'"

It wasn't exactly putting Cubs brass in the best of situations. Here was one of their best pitchers—the Cy Young winner in

1984—offering part of his salary while the team was scrambling to figure out how to deal with this player and his agent appearing at camp without warning. "I got a handwritten letter from Dallas Green, telling me that he wanted Andre more than me, but his hands were being tied," Sutcliffe said. "And actually that letter went a long way toward the collusion agreement that the players got. He basically admitted what was going on, and I love him to death for it."

Later, Green would credit Dawson's agent, Moss, with a good "PR campaign," according to the *Chicago Tribune*. "I didn't like it at all," Green said to him. "You put us in a position where you got everybody in Chicago excited. You got everybody on the team excited, and there was no way we could say no."

So Dawson and Moss got their meeting. And to put even more pressure on the team, the player and agent made an even more unprecedented move, which would go down in baseball history: Dawson offered to play for a blank check. They told Green to fill in the amount. There was *no* negotiation. "I told him, 'We're not here to negotiate with you. I feel that I can help the team,'" Dawson said. "'Fill in the blanks. Pay me what you think I'm worth. We're not here to waste your time. I want to be real brief about it, but I do want you to understand that I'm only going to leave it on the table for 24 hours.'"

Remember, Dawson also had the Braves to visit next. He figured one of the two teams would accept his offer, but he couldn't just allow them to delay. He needed a *little* leverage. He didn't have much. "Dallas didn't really know what to make of it," Dawson recalled with a laugh. "His comeback was that he had young players that he needed to give a look and give an opportunity to try to make the ballclub, which I understood."

In fact, Green, who passed away in 2017, was just stalling because he really didn't know how to handle such an unusual

THE FRANCHISE: CHICAGO CUBS

situation. "He said something like, 'Let my legal team look it over, and I'll get back to you as soon as I can,'" Dawson said. "So we left Arizona. I went back home to Florida."

Dawson had made it clear that the offer would expire the next day. He also planned that visit to Braves camp. It was a high stakes game of poker, but at least Dawson had players and fans on his side. "Handing them the blank contract and saying you fill out the amount was pretty special," Maddux said. "No one had done that. We wanted him on our team."

The next day Green called Dawson and offered him $500,000. His salary the season before was over $1 million. "It was less than what Montreal was offering," Dawson said. "I understood it as an offer for me to refuse."

Green was calling Dawson's bluff—if he was bluffing in the first place, of course. Would he really play for less than half of what he was making the previous season? It gave the general manager an out if Dawson turned it down. After saying he'd play for anything and then saying no when there was an offer on the table, perhaps the Cubs would come out of the situation looking like they had been honorable.

Except Dawson said yes. "He got quiet," Dawson recalled. "He didn't really say anything for about 15 seconds, and I thought I actually lost the call. And I said, 'Hello?' And he said, 'I'm here. Can I call you back in about an hour?'"

It's further evidence Green was surprised by the answer. Otherwise he would have told Dawson to get on a plane, sign the contract, and start spring training. Eventually, Green did call back and welcomed Dawson to the Cubs. The blank check approach worked—so to speak. Dawson had a job just not for nearly as much as he was worth. "Andre and Dick were willing to sacrifice salary and principle in 1987 to play in Wrigley Field for the Cubs," Green said in a statement after Dawson agreed to the contract. "He was willing to bet that his production on the field would better his salary for 1988 and the future—something rather unusual in itself in these wild days of free agency."

Green could never know how right he would be. After all the offseason drama came to its conclusion, Dawson still had to perform on the field. His first year in Chicago would be memorable. In fact, it turned out to be one of the best in Cubs history. "I felt total respect for him," Maddux said. "After signing that contract, it was all about baseball for him. If we were on the field, stretching and taking batting practice, I would just say to him that I had total respect. I definitely respected the way that he performed after signing the contract. He was terrific. He was more than terrific."

Dawson started the 1987 season a little slow. He was just eight for his first 51 (a .157 average) but would soon find his footing. He may have been on a mission to prove the baseball world wrong after his phone didn't ring much during the winter, but he also had other personal motivation for having a good first season in Chicago. "I lost my grandmother early in the year, during the offseason actually," Dawson said. "And to me, my grandmother was my role model growing up. She was not my grandmother but my mother in a sense. I was the oldest of eight siblings, so my grandmother was the one that kind of coached me about life challenges and how do you avoid trouble in a sense. So losing her really affected me. I think the toughest thing I ever had to do in life at that time was to close her coffin."

Dawson dedicated the season to his grandmother and then dedicated himself to the game. He didn't analyze or think beyond each day. He lived in the moment. "For the first time, I didn't really set any goals," Dawson explained. "I just said, 'I'm going to have as much fun as I can and just let natural ability run its course.' I actually got off to a slow start. I was pressing a bit early, maybe perhaps trying to fit in to the scheme of things there. But I knew I didn't have to feel my way around. It was just a matter of adjusting to the new environment. And it took a grand slam home run off of Todd Worrell and St. Louis that really got me rolling and got me going."

That moment came on April 22 and instantly began a long-term love affair with an entire fanbase. The Cubs had beaten the St. Louis Cardinals 5–4 the day before but were down 3–1 in the seventh inning when Worrell took the ball in relief. The bases were loaded but not for long, as Dawson unloaded and sent a pitch into the left-field stands. The Cubs beat the Cardinals again that day 5–4. "From there, it just appeared that things just started to happen on a day-to-day basis," Dawson said. "I was so at peace that year, enjoying Chicago and the fanbase."

The grand slam occurred in St. Louis, and then two days later, he returned to Montreal and torched his former team. Dawson had seven hits and six RBIs against the Expos in the three-game series. By the time the Cubs returned to Wrigley Field, Dawson was a beloved player. Fans made him feel like he was one of theirs. "They embraced me from Day One," Dawson said. "And when they started Andre's Army and they started salaaming [bowing down to] me in the outfield, it was just something that was so overwhelming that I just had to enjoy it each and every day."

It became a daily tradition. Dawson would do something special at the plate and when he returned to the outfield the next inning the fans in the right-field bleachers would start bowing down to him out of respect. He quickly went on a nine-game hit streak, and his MVP caliber season was off and running.

Sutcliffe explained his success. "Being on grass and playing during the day gave him a chance to be healthier," he said.

"With night games there's not a lot of times after the game to ice your knees and stuff. You want to get home. The schedule at Wrigley worked for him. And that was some unbelievable baseball that he was playing."

From outfield assists to running the bases to his massive power, Dawson arguably equaled Sutcliffe and even former MVP Sandberg in popularity. And his presence at the plate was intimidating.

Though the Cubs would eventually finish in last place in the National League East that season, they were still over .500 as spring gave way to the summer months. Dawson was in the midst of his best season; he already had 20 home runs by July 1. After playing the San Francisco Giants over the July 4 holiday, the Cubs welcomed the San Diego Padres to town for two games.

Back then, there was still some lingering animosity between the teams—or at least by Cubs fans—as only three years prior, the Padres had knocked the Cubs from the postseason despite trailing 2–0 in the best-of-five series. It was a heartbreaking defeat. So any chance at revenge—even years later—was savored.

In the first game of the series on July 6, Dawson hit two home runs and drove in four in a 7–0 Cubs win. The sun-drenched fans in the right-field bleachers were ecstatic and showed their appreciation often. "I was going well at that point in the season," Dawson said. "They appreciated it."

The next day all hell would break loose not long after Dawson hit another home run—this time off Padres starter Eric Show. The Cubs were hitting Show pretty well and by the bottom of the third inning—when Dawson came to the plate again—they led 4–2. That's when Show decided to come inside on Dawson. *Way inside.* Show's second pitch hit Dawson in the face. He went down, gushing blood. Led by Sutcliffe, who went right after Show, the benches cleared. "As a player you are aware of when things are intentional and when they're not," Dawson told PBS in a television interview. "You can't convince any of those players it wasn't a purposeful knock-down pitch."

The scene was wild. Sutcliffe and others attacked Show while Dawson lay on the ground. Then after getting up, Dawson—bloody face and all—went after the pitcher. Eventually, Show ran into the Padres clubhouse, and things settled down. Sutcliffe explained what got him so upset. "When I was a rookie, Davey Lopes told me to drill Manny Trillo," Sutcliffe explained. "He was getting too comfortable at the plate. Then Dusty Baker tells me that Steve Carlton is going to retaliate, but the first pitch was a breaking ball in the dirt. He let me get comfortable. The next pitch went between my helmet and my head. He *wanted* to get me."

Sutcliffe viewed that as crossing a line. Show did the same thing to Dawson: throwing a pitch outside before drilling him. He allowed the Cubs star to believe he was going to be okay, though Sutcliffe remembers warning his teammate anyway. "Andre was getting ready to walk up to home plate, and I stopped him—and I never did this before and I never did it again. I said, 'Hawk, I got a bad feeling here, buddy. I don't know why, but I just have to tell you that.' And he goes, 'I know. I'm going to take a look at the first pitch.'"

After that first pitch went low away, Sutcliffe remembered the incident with Carlton and was still on high alert. "And I'm at the top step," Sutcliffe said, "and all of a sudden, I see him wind up and I saw him look at Hawk's head and I just screamed."

Said Dawson: "I was convinced he was trying to knock me down, but when you throw up and in, there's a fine line."

Days later, the fracas would end up on the cover of *Sports Illustrated* with a picture of Dawson just as he was getting hit by the ball. His status grew even more after he had gotten off the ground and chased Show into the visitors' clubhouse. He was the victim, but Dawson also showed grit and toughness. America—not just Chicago—fell for him.

For some players, a beaning like the one Dawson got that day might impact them for weeks, months, or even years. It's not easy to step back into the batter's box after getting hit in the face. But Hawk missed just a couple games and got right back to his MVP season. Dawson compiled a .913 OPS in the month of July while hitting eight home runs, though he went nine games without a long ball after getting hit in the face. Who knows? Without the beaning perhaps Dawson gets to 50 on the season. Nevertheless, he had 28 home runs as the calendar flipped to August. It was a huge number at that time.

The Cubs were hosting the Philadelphia Phillies on that first day of the new month. The teams were fierce, divisional competitors and in that moment were separated by just a game in the standings. The Cubs featured Dawson while the Phillies had slugger Mike Schmidt. "I had finished runner-up to the MVP award twice in Montreal," Dawson said, "once to Dale Murphy and once to Mike Schmidt. And I could have very easily won that award both of those years. Well, I won't say easily, but I could have won that award, but I realized I wasn't going to win it playing across the border in Montreal. You just don't get that kind of exposure."

Dawson was getting plenty of exposure now. And here he was late in the season going up against Schmidt who was having another good year of his own. Schmidt had 22 home runs to Dawson's 28 as they both took the field that day. It was hot and humid, but that didn't stop the Cubs right fielder. About three hours later, Dawson's home run total rose to 31. He hit three. "I was tired, but the heat and humidity helped," he said at the time, according to the *Chicago Tribune*. "When you're tired, the bat feels heavy, and it helps cut down on your swing. You can get your hands into it more."

Dawson drove in all five runs in a 5–3 win, getting standing ovations and curtain calls along the way, while Schmidt did little. He went 1-for-5, watching Dawson put yet another stamp on his MVP season. In fact, he may have won it that day. "I put up a pretty incredible year," Dawson said, "the best year I could have imagined. So at that point, I'm thinking maybe I'll be considered again with those who are up for the award."

Dawson's home run total kept rising as the final month of the season approached. He had 43 by September 1, but a 10-game homerless stretch to begin the month put a real dent in him being able to reach 50. No one had hit at least that many in the NL since George Foster in 1977. Dawson had 48 as the team played its final series of the season—in Montreal of all places. He hit just one home run in the three games, finishing his first season in Chicago with 49 to go along with 137 runs driven in, and a .287 batting average. He even stole 11 bases. It was a mammoth year. "I was able to see it firsthand from the dugout to the locker room, pregame/postgame, all of it," Sandberg said. "I was on base when he was hitting the 49 home runs, which in today's game would be more like 59 or 60. He was just hitting them so often. It was incredible to watch."

When it came time to vote for the MVP, it was no sure thing Dawson would win it. He played for a team that finished in last place, as the Cubs ended up 76–85 in 1987. And though there was no rule preventing voters from choosing him for that reason, some thought it could have an impact. To this day, only two players (Dawson and Alex Rodriguez) have won the MVP on a last-place team.

In the end, Dawson beat out Cardinals teammates Ozzie Smith and Jack Clark. The best regular-season team in the NL took a backseat to the Cubs right fielder who months earlier signed a blank check to play for $500,000 while earning $200,000 more in incentives. The Cubs got their money's worth and then some. "He could do it all," Sutcliffe said. "We can talk about his offense, but he saved runs. Guys wouldn't run on him. Pitchers loved when he was out there. It was one of the best years I've ever seen. He earned that award."

The postscript to the 1987 season is that Dawson once again needed a new contract. Amazingly, one wasn't just handed to him. "I wasn't extended and I was kind of puzzled at the prospect of arbitration because they had the ability to sign me for a while going forward," Dawson said.

Arbitration is where a third-party expert decides a salary for a player instead of player and team negotiating one. It can be a messy process. "We were asking for two million, and they were offering $1.8 million. And you just don't go to arbitration when you're that close," Dawson said. "You settle somewhere in between, and it didn't happen."

Nothing was going to come easy for Dawson at this point, but he was used to fighting for everything he had gotten from this game. Incredibly, Dawson lost his arbitration case, but the new season was nearing, and the last thing the Cubs wanted was an unhappy star. They changed their tune. "They were told not to piss me off in arbitration because spring training was just a couple of weeks away," Dawson said. "We get the arbitration process done, we get the spring training, and then out of nowhere, I'm extended another three years."

Dawson got $6 million for three years. He finally got his payday. From showing up uninvited to winning the MVP to losing an arbitration case to finally getting some security, it capped an incredibly dramatic 12-month period for one of the game's best players. Dawson arrived in Chicago in 1987, but his landing was anything but smooth. "I took it all in stride up until the point that we lost the arbitration case," Dawson said. "I won't say that I was bitter. I just had very ill feelings about the process itself. Then I got the extension. But that first year is something I'll never forget. Cubs fans welcomed me, and I had my best season. You don't play this game for money. I think that's why I had such a good year. I just loved being a Cub."

3

Sammy Sosa

ON THE NIGHT BEFORE LABOR DAY IN 1998, A PAIR OF BUSES
inched their way toward the Marriott Hotel in downtown
St. Louis. On one of those buses rode Chicago Cubs players.
On the other were the manager, coaches, staff members, and
writers who hopped a ride aboard the team's charter flight from
Pittsburgh after a Sunday afternoon game so they could get to
St. Louis in time for a Monday afternoon holiday game between
the Cubs and the St. Louis Cardinals.

The scene outside the buses was extraordinary. Fans of the
Cubs and fans of their Gateway Arch rivals, the Cardinals, lined
the sidewalks three and four deep. Everybody wanted to get a
glimpse of Sammy Sosa, who was locked in a historic home run
duel with the Cardinals' Mark McGwire. Even though Sosa was
in enemy territory, it was as if the pope or The Beatles were
coming to town. "Traveling with a rock star," recalled Sharon
Pannozzo, then the Cubs' director of media relations and the

person who deftly managed Sosa after he burst onto the national scene by hitting 20 home runs in June and then cheerfully battling the dour McGwire as both men took aim at Roger Maris' single-season record for home runs (61) set in 1961.

This was the grandest of grand entrances. Yes, Sosa had arrived—in so many ways.

The next day, Sosa and McGwire held a joint news conference under a tent at Busch Stadium. The very idea of two opposing players meeting the media together might have been unthinkable, but these were unprecedented times. Before a national media throng, Sosa ate up the attention. All summer long during the home run duel, Sosa constantly and consistently referred to McGwire as "The Man." So during the joint news conference, one intrepid beat writer stood up and said, "Once and for all, which one of you is 'The Man?'"

Sosa didn't miss beat. "He is 'The Man' in the United States," he said of McGwire. "I am 'The Man' in the Dominican Republic."

The answer was perfect, and it brought the house down.

McGwire hit home runs No. 61 and 62 during the two-game series to tie and break Maris' record. He ended the season with 70 homers, while Sosa hit 66 and helped the Cubs win the National League wild-card.

The 1998 season was the beginning of a mostly beautiful seven-year run for Sosa. That run ended on the final day of the 2004 season. If the entrance in 1998 was grand, the exit in '04 was ignominious, ending in hurt feelings and bitterness on both Sosa's side and that of the Cubs.

Sosa was traded to the Baltimore Orioles before the 2005 season. He exited the Cubs as their all-time leading home-run hitter with 545. He wound up with 609 for his career. Despite those numbers and the pleasure Sosa brought to so many fans, his career ended in a cloud of suspicion over possible use of performance-enhancing drugs. His messy exit from the Cubs and the current ownership's unwillingness to welcome him back to his beloved Chicago also muddies the waters, as do whispers of him being "selfish" and a "bad teammate."

Despite his numbers and no doubt because of the PED suspicion, Sosa did not come close to election to the Hall of Fame. The highest percentage of votes he garnered in 10 years on the ballot—with 75 percent needed from the Baseball Writers Association of America—was 18.5.

So the question is this: what is Sammy Sosa's ultimate legacy as a Chicago Cub and in baseball history? The answer is this: it's complicated, really complicated.

* * *

Most fans are familiar with Sammy Sosa's life story. He was born near San Pedro de Macoris in the Dominican Republic on November 12, 1968. San Pedro de Macoris long has been considered a cradle of baseball players. Living in abject poverty, Sosa shined shoes to help his family make ends meet.

The Texas Rangers signed him in 1985, and he made his major league debut on June 16, 1989, going 2-for-4 at Yankee Stadium. He hit his first big league homer in his sixth career game on June 21 against Roger Clemens of the Boston Red Sox at Fenway Park.

Coming up, Sosa was the proverbial five-tool player, one who could hit, hit for power, run, field, and throw. During his career Sosa would show flashes of all five tools, but he would be known primarily as a power hitter during his most productive seasons.

One person who saw potential in Sosa was Larry Himes, the general manager of the Chicago White Sox from October of 1986 through the 1990 season. Himes is best known as the executive who rebuilt a barren White Sox farm system with the likes of Frank Thomas, Jack McDowell, Alex Fernandez, Robin Ventura, and Jason Bere. Enticed by the potential he saw in Sosa, Himes pulled off a shocker of a trade on July 29, 1989, when he dealt future Hall of Famer Harold Baines along with infielder Fred Manrique to the Rangers for Sosa, pitcher Wilson Alvarez, and infielder Scott Fletcher.

Baines, who was drafted first overall by former White Sox owner Bill Veeck in 1977, was not only a fan favorite, but also a valued teammate in the clubhouse with both the players and with manager Jeff Torborg. Jerry Reinsdorf, the White Sox' chairman, was so emotionally attached to Baines that he retired his uniform number weeks after the trade was made. "What people forget is that it was probably the most controversial trade the Sox ever made," said Mark Ruda, the beat writer covering the White Sox for the *Daily Herald* from 1986 through the 1993 season after having covered the Cubs. "Harold was an icon outsized of what he did. Politically, it was a tough move to the point where Reinsdorf, [team president Eddie] Einhorn, the whole brain trust put the scouts on the spot. Basically the scouting brain trust was asked, I believe by Einhorn, 'Are you willing to risk your jobs on this trade?' And they all said yes. This was back when scouts made baseball writer salaries. They all risked their livelihoods. Not that most of them couldn't get other jobs, but still if you're unemployed, it's going to hurt you more than the average baseball player. They risked their jobs on this thing because it was Harold Frickin' Baines."

The White Sox were going nowhere in 1989 and they finished the season with a record of 69–92—good for last place in the American League West. The Baines–Sosa trade was seen as move for the future, a future that arrived in 1990, when they finished with a record of 94–68 and battled the mighty Oakland A's all summer long before winding up in second place. The future was of little interest to those in the Chicago clubhouse when Baines was traded. "You would have thought that Harold had died," Ruda said. "[First baseman Greg] Walker especially, [reliever Bobby] Thigpen, everybody, was mourning it. It did not go down well in the clubhouse. Who was GM? Larry Himes, who had a couple years earlier had banned beer in the clubhouse. Carlton Fisk referred to Harold as, 'My best friend.'"

As a GM, whether with the White Sox or later the Cubs, Himes was not a beloved figure among players. In addition to banning beer in the clubhouse, Himes insisted players wear socks on road trips. Former White Sox Rookie of the Year Ron Kittle said Himes had all the charm of a pet rock. The trade of Baines did little to help his popularity. "Larry Himes was a disliked person," Ruda said. "Upstairs in Larry's [hotel] suite, he calls in Torborg and tells him about the trade. He totally blindsides Torborg to the point where Torborg never let on after that how mad he was. But he was livid because they totally blindsided him. Look, Torborg was astute enough to know this was not going to play well in the clubhouse. So, Torborg, being Torborg, probably would have gotten his brain trust together— [coaches] Joe Nossek, Sammy Ellis, et al. Knowing Torborg like I knew him, he probably would have done some damage control ahead of time, maybe planting the seed of, 'Look, we might have changes coming down. You might not like it. Be prepared at least.' It was a big deal. I think that, even though Himes hired Torborg, it ruined their relationship to when Larry was fired, Jeff certainly didn't say, 'Good riddance.' That wasn't Torborg. He was Mr. Political. He didn't even shed a single crocodile tear, which was very telling to me. Torborg was probably thinking, *I'll roll the dice with whoever they hire at this point, and we'll go from there.* But that forever ruined the relationship between Torborg and Himes in my opinion."

Himes seemed to know what the reaction would be when he made the trade. "It's an unpopular decision as far as Sox fans are concerned," he told the *Chicago Tribune* at the time. "It doesn't mean that it isn't a good decision. This is a decision we made as far as direction of the Chicago White Sox for today and for our future."

Sosa played 13 games with the White Sox' Triple A Vancouver affiliate in 1989 before being called up to the big club. In 33 games with the White Sox, he put up a line of .273/.351/.414 with three home runs, 10 RBIs, seven stolen bases, and 27 strikeouts in 115 plate appearances. He spent the entire 1990 season with the White Sox, compiling line of .233/.282/.404 with 15 homers, 70 RBIs, 32 stolen bases, and 150 strikeouts in 579 plate appearances. He was sent back to Vancouver for 32 games in 1991 and wound up with a line in Chicago of .203/.240/.335 with 10 homers, 33 RBIs, and 98 strikeouts in 338 plate appearances.

By that time, Himes had moved to the North Side of Chicago to run the Cubs' baseball operations, having been replaced by the White Sox with Ron Schueler. Clearly something wasn't clicking with Sosa and the White Sox. The biggest problem was the relationship between Sosa and hitting coach Walt Hriniak, a gruff, cigar-smoking authoritarian. Hriniak, a .253 hitter in 47 major league games, was a disciple of hitting coach Charlie Lau, whose claim to fame was mentoring George Brett during Brett's chase of a .400 batting average in 1980 as a member of the Kansas City Royals. Lau later was hired by the White Sox, but he died in 1984.

Hriniak taught Lau's hitting style, which called for the batter to keep his head down and release the top hand on the bat upon contact with the ball. It was a method that worked for Brett and White Sox Hall of Famer Thomas but not for Sosa, who chafed like a wild stallion under the tutelage of Hriniak. The White Sox were ready to give up on Sosa as Himes watched with more than casual interest from the North Side.

On March 30, 1992, at the end of spring training, Himes struck again, acquiring Sosa and pitcher Ken Patterson from the White Sox in exchange for 32-year-old slugger George Bell, who enjoyed his best days with the Toronto Blue Jays and was seen as a known commodity. As for Sosa, he was still an unknown, and his relationship with Hriniak didn't help matters. "There were storm clouds all around this guy but a lot of potential, a lot of flashes," Ruda said. "You could see what the scouts saw in him but enigmatic, sporadic, up and down. I think the coaching staff had some problems with him. The Hriniak stuff, truth be told, a lot of players had problems with Hriniak. The odd thing is: I don't recall Thomas being as outspoken a fan of Hriniak as he is now. If Sammy bristled under the Hriniak hitting style, so did a lot of people. And it went down through their whole organization, where every hitting coach in the minors was a Walt Hriniak clone. You had to do it the Walt way or the highway basically. A lot of them ended up taking the highway. Thomas became a Hall of Famer while adopting some of it. God bless. Good. But even the best hitting coaches tell you it's not one way is the only way."

Bell was a prickly figure with staff members and the media. Those covering the White Sox would find that out. Meanwhile, the Cubs seemed to welcome Sosa with open arms. "First of all, in my mind, I was not a George Bell fan," former Cubs media relations director Sharon Pannozzo said. "So when Larry Himes made that trade, I could not have been happier. I went into Larry Himes and said that's the best trade anybody has ever made. And I didn't even know that much about Sammy Sosa at the time. I just did not like George Bell. He was not a good person for the clubhouse. As I recall, Sammy, just a very affable guy. He was really, quite honestly for those years before '98, pretty low-key. He was just a guy in the clubhouse doing his job. He wasn't this big personality. Easy to work with, always willing to do whatever you asked, just a very affable guy, I enjoyed him."

Bell played only two years with the White Sox before retiring. In those two years, Bell's Wins Above Replacement was minus-2.7. Truth be told, he was a drag on the 1993 team, which won the American League West. His batting line in '93 was .217/.243/.363 with 13 home runs and 64 RBIs. By contrast, Sosa's WAR with the White Sox in parts of three seasons was a positive 1.1. In 13 years with the Cubs, Sosa's cumulative WAR was 58.8.

For all the flak the Cubs get for their 1964 trade of future Hall of Famer Lou Brock to the St. Louis Cardinals for sore-armed pitcher Ernie Broglio, they made up for it by trading Bell for Sosa. With his new Cubs team, Sosa had a front-office backer in Himes, and that may have caused some resentment among veteran players, who came to dislike their GM as much as players on the White Sox did. Some even saw Sosa as Himes' special project or teacher's pet.

Sosa's 1992 season with the Cubs was just so-so, but he flashed his overall abilities in 1993, joining the 30/30 club with 33 home runs and 36 stolen bases. He would enjoy another 30/30 season in 1995. The idea of Sosa fulfilling his potential as a five-tool player was becoming a reality.

One interesting aside that many people may have forgotten is that Sosa could have become a member of the Boston Red Sox during the 1994–95 players' strike, which wiped out the end of the '94 season as well as the postseason. During the strike the owners implemented a system that made 38 players with four or five years of experience restricted free agents. If a player signed with a team, his old team would have 10 days to match the contract. The Red Sox had reached agreements with Sosa, Kevin Appier of the Royals, and John Wetteland of the Montreal Expos. But a ruling by the National Labor Relations Board overturned that system and Sosa remained a Cub.

The 1996 season was shaping up to be a historic one for Sammy Sosa. Then on August 20 in a game against the Florida Marlins at Wrigley Field, Sosa was hit on the right wrist by a pitch from Mark Hutton in the first inning. Sosa remained in the game, as was his wont. Whatever his faults, Sosa was a gamer. He never wanted to come out of a game and he never wanted a day off. The August 20 game was the 124th of the season for the Cubs and the 124th of the season for Sosa. The pain in Sosa's wrist became too great to bear, and he left the game after popping out in the fourth inning. The next day, he and the Cubs got the bad news. Sosa had suffered a fractured pisiforme bone just above the right wrist. Sosa would miss the rest of the season. The Cubs were 62–62 at the time of the injury. They would finish the season 76–86. "After I got hit, my feeling was that I was hurt, but I wasn't hurt that bad," Sosa told the *Daily Herald*. "I could feel it later and I said to Johnny [athletic trainer Fierro] to take me out of the game. When I went back home, I couldn't sleep. It was hurting me bad. About the only way I can't play is if something is broken."

Cubs general manager Ed Lynch's words showed how much Sosa meant to the Cubs, even then. "I'm not going to lie to you: it's the most disappointing news I've gotten in my professional career," Lynch said. "I've come to take Sammy for granted in the lineup seven days a week."

Sosa finished the year with 40 home runs and 100 RBIs. He was on pace for 52 homers and 131 RBIs. In 1997 Sosa came back and played in all 162 games, putting up a line of .251/.300/.480 with 36 home runs, 119 RBIs, and 22 stolen bases for a team that started the season 0–14 on the way to a 68–94 record. But on the final weekend of the season, Sosa ran afoul of manager Jim Riggleman and GM Lynch for ignoring a hold sign and getting caught trying to steal second base. Riggleman upbraided Sosa in front of the team. Later, Riggleman and Lynch urged Sosa to become more of a team player.

Interviewed in 2022, Riggleman was magnanimous toward Sosa. "In '97 at the end of the year, Sammy ran when he shouldn't have run," he said, "Sammy never made an excuse about it. I got on him pretty good. I loved Sammy. Sammy treated me with great respect. I got on him and I felt I had to do it because the other players saw him run when they knew he shouldn't have run. I did not realize at the time that he was trying to get his 200th [career] stolen base. That should not be the determining factor, but at least I could understand later what he was doing. I got on him pretty good. The next spring, the first few days of spring training, he wouldn't even talk to me. So I went up to him, and I said, 'What are you going to do? You're never going to talk to me again?' And then he gave me a big hug, and we were good."

* * *

The 1998 Chicago Cubs season was a whirlwind before it even started, and Sammy Sosa didn't even enter the big picture until June. Just as spring training was starting, beloved broadcaster Harry Caray died. Caray knew Sosa was the box office. During telecasts he would tell TV director Arne Harris, "Arne, get the camera on Sammy!"

One star who was emerging in Mesa, Arizona, was a fresh-faced pitcher name Kerry Wood. Despite dazzling teammates and foes like in the Cactus League, Wood began the season at Triple A Iowa before coming up in April. On May 6 he tied a major league record by striking out 20 batters against the Houston Astros.

As for Sosa, he was meandering through a routine early season. At one point in mid-May, he even refused to talk with beat reporters in Cincinnati. He said nothing was wrong, that he just didn't want to talk about himself. Sosa entered June with 13 home runs, having hit two in games on May 25 and May 27. Perhaps that should have warned us.

Sosa had another two-homer game on June 1. His first that day came off future teammate and then-Florida Marlins pitcher Ryan Dempster, who was making his first major league start. When June had ended, Sosa had set a major league record with 20 home runs. He entered July with 33, and life would never be the same again—for anyone around Sosa.

Sosa became a national celebrity, and the Cubs were in a playoff chase. While Mark McGwire did interviews grudgingly—he had 37 homers by the end of June—Sosa relished the attention. He also deferred to McGwire, calling him "The Man" at every turn. Sharon Pannozzo handled Sosa's media availabilities masterfully. TV and radio reporters talked to Sosa at his locker first followed by the print media. In those days the Cubs had no interview room. All postgame interviews—including those of manager Jim Riggleman—were done in the cramped Wrigley Field clubhouse. "Honestly, I'll credit Sammy for a lot of it because Sammy was a very willing participant who was embracing the experience and enjoying it," Pannozzo said. "It made my job easier. I want to tell you: there was a lot coming at us. He was such a professional. It was just a matter of trying to find time to schedule everything and making him available because he wanted to be available. He was very happy to talk to the media. He liked the media. He had a very engaging way about him. From my perspective, that certainly made my job easier. Sammy enjoyed every minute of it. He loved the attention. He loved the fact that people were recognizing his accomplishments. And he just had fun, literally had fun. It was not a chore to him. My perspective and my observation of Mark [McGwire] during those times was that it was a job. It was what he was being asked to do, and he did it. It wasn't like he took any of the joy out of it. Sammy had joy. Sammy was experiencing a lot of new attention and he embraced it."

By the time the Cubs arrived in St. Louis for Labor Day, Sosa had 58 home runs; McGwire had 60. Maris' record wasn't just going to be broken; it was going to be obliterated. McGwire tied Maris at 61 on Labor Day with a first-inning homer off Mike Morgan. The next night, he broke the record with No. 62 on a line-drive homer to left against Steve Trachsel in the fourth. As the St. Louis Cardinals and 43,688 fans at Busch Stadium celebrated, Sosa ran in from right field to embrace "The Man." Sammy was going to show everybody he was a good sport, and if the photographers got him into the photo with the star of the night, all the better.

McGwire won the home run title with 70, and Sosa finished with 66. With the Cubs capturing the wild-card, Sosa easily won the Most Valuable Player award in the National League, and both players appeared on the cover of *Sports Illustrated* dressed in togas.

Storm clouds were brewing, however, and they had to do with the specter of performance-enhancing drugs. In August of 1998, a reporter from the Associated Press spotted a bottle of androstenedione in McGwire's locker. "Andro," as it was known, is a testosterone-producing pill that was not banned by Major League Baseball at the time. "I remember there was a Sunday night game—Cubs and Cardinals," said Cubs radio broadcaster Pat Hughes, who called all of Sosa's homers in 1998. "And one of the ESPN people, either one of the announcers or producers said, 'Hey, did you hear about McGwire testing positive for androstenedione?' I said, 'A, I did not hear it, and B, I have no idea what that is.' To this day, I don't know if in those days they were injecting themselves, taking pills, liquids, powders. I have no idea. That complicates it because of my lack of knowledge of who was doing what, what was illegal, what was legal at the time if any of it."

Sosa had come to spring training of 1998 noticeably bigger than he had been. During the season and in subsequent years, he attributed his newfound strength to "Flintstones vitamins." He also was an extremely hard worker both the in the weight room and in the batting cage. "Spring training was a shock," Cubs batting coach Jeff Pentland told the *Daily Herald* in June of 1998. Pentland joined the Cubs during the 1997 season and immediately hit it off with Sosa. "I didn't realize how good he was until I saw him in spring training. He hadn't done anything in the Dominican other than get himself in shape. He came out and the first day he was smoking. I was shocked at how quick his bat was, how quick he really was. My thing was, *Gee, we got to try to get this thing to work right because there's an awful lot of talent.*"

Sosa hit 63 home runs in 1999, but the Cubs crashed to a record of 67–95, and Riggleman was fired and replaced by Don Baylor, an outstanding hitter in the major leagues during his playing days and the manager of the Colorado Rockies from their inception in 1993 through 1998. During spring training of 2000, Sosa said Baylor knew how to handle superstars, citing his time with Larry Walker in Colorado. But the two suffered a major falling out during the season, and Sosa was nearly traded during the summer. During spring training Baylor said he wanted Sosa to become a more complete player like the one who displayed the five tools that had scouts drooling early in his career. As Sosa became a power hitter, the other parts of his game took a back seat. He no longer was stealing bases and he became somewhat of an indifferent fielder. Sosa blasted Baylor for a lack of respect. The two patched things up, but the Cubs actively looked to trade him.

A deal with the New York Yankees looked like it might happen in June, but it fell through at the last minute. Sosa was going to stay with the Cubs. Still, there were scars. For all the fame and money Sosa had attained, he always seemed to be seeking something more. "I don't think that he felt that he was totally accepted by some of his teammates," said Mike Kiley, the Cubs beat writer for the *Chicago Sun-Times* from 1997 to 2006. Kiley was the media person Sosa trusted the most, and he often would confide in the veteran scribe. "Of course, a lot of the Latin players were his friends, but as far as having the whole [locker] room on his side, I think he struggled with that a little bit. He didn't see a way to sometimes to win everybody over. People are going to say, 'Yeah, well, what about the boom box?' That, obviously, wasn't one of his great PR moves: to have the boom box and playing music. But, again, he thought he was at that point the star in his mind and whatever he wanted to do should be okay with others. He made some errors in judgment in some of those moves. He was sensitive. If he saw a slight, a perceived slight or a real slight, he didn't mind coming out and saying, 'Hey, this isn't right. They shouldn't be going after me like this. I'm really one of the best players here.'"

Sosa hit 50 homers in 2000 for a club that finished 65–97. Armed with a contract extension and seemingly happy in 2001, Sosa hit 64 home runs, drove in 160 runs, and had an OPS of 1.174 for a club that contended until September before falling out of the race. It was really a season for ages. "You never saw anything like that," said Ron Coomer, a member of the 2001 Cubs and the current team's radio analyst. "I never played with a guy that good. Sixty home runs, driving in runs. I would hit in the cage usually right after him. Watching him work and what he was able to do with his swing was incredible with the extreme power and with the repetition. He could step and repeat the same great swing over and over and over. That was something we just didn't see. There were only a few. Griffey Jr. was one. There were only a few. [Sosa] and Bonds and McGwire were able to do that eventually."

Sosa was a fan favorite for years at Wrigley Field and he served up a master symbolic stroke after the Cubs returned to play their first home series after the September 11, 2001, terrorist attacks on the United States. The Cubs honored first responders with a stirring pregame ceremony, and buildings around the ballpark were festooned with large American flags. Sosa came to bat in the bottom of the first inning and hit a home run. Before he reached first base, he was handed a small American flag by coach Billy Williams. Sosa rounded the bases with the flag in his hand. It was the perfect moment. "A lot of people don't know how he got that flag," Williams said in 2018. "After 9/11 we came back to play and, of course, we had it planned because he was hitting home runs so frequently. The wind was blowing in that night. I didn't think the ball was going to go out. I had the flag down in my sock. When Sammy hit the home run, I was looking at the ball out in right field, and Sammy was getting close. The wind was blowing in, and Sammy was getting close. I was looking at the ball again. I had to reach down quick and give it to him. By that time, the people had [followed] the ball. They didn't see me give Sammy the flag. It was really neat. When he ran around the bases, he had the flag in his hand. After the game I got Sammy to sign the flag and I still have it at home."

Baylor was fired in the middle of the 2002 season, in which the Cubs limped home under interim manager Bruce Kimm for a season total of 67–95. Sosa led the National League in home runs with 49 in an otherwise drab season. Cubs general manager Jim Hendry hired Dusty Baker to manage the club late in 2002, and the team won the National League Central in 2003 with a record of 88–74. But for Sosa 2003 was a mixed bag and in hindsight it probably spelled the beginning of the end of his time as a Cub. On Sunday, April 20, in a game at Pittsburgh's PNC Park, Sosa homered against Josh Fogg in the first inning. Leading off the fourth inning against Pirates pitcher Salomon Torres, Sosa was hit in the head with a pitch. The impact shattered Sosa's batting helmet, and the sound of ball hitting plastic could be heard high up in the press box. Sosa left the game and was taken to a hospital for precautionary reasons. He returned to the park later and flew home on the team's charter. After an off day in the schedule, Sosa was back in the lineup for the team's next game, which occurred against the San Diego Padres on April 22. The beaning was a frightening-looking play, and some observers felt it affected Sosa, causing him to move farther away from home plate in the batter's box.

Then, on June 3, during a game against the Tampa Bay Devil Rays at Wrigley Field, Sosa broke his bat while grounding out in the first inning. The Devils Rays showed the bat to umpires, who ejected Sosa from the game for having cork in the barrel of the bat. Sosa was called a cheater, and it had nothing to do with steroids. One story goes that the Cubs got a phone call that night from Major League Baseball warning them that representatives were on their way to inspect all Cubs bats. If there were any other corked bats, the Cubs had a heads-up to get rid of them. The Cubs and Sosa said that he used the corked bat by mistake, that it was one he was using in batting practice to entertain fans with long blasts. Few were buying that story, and Sosa wound up with a seven-game suspension. One Cubs insider postulated at the time that Sosa was using a corked bat to jump-start his season after the beaning in Pittsburgh.

Both Sosa and the Cubs recovered, and Baker's boys went on to win the NL Central. Sosa wound up with 40 homers and 103 RBIs, and all looked rosy after the Cubs won their first postseason series since 1908, as they upset the Atlanta Braves in five games of the National League Division Series, during which Sosa went only 3-for-16. The Cubs looked like they were headed to their first World Series since 1945 when they took a three-games-to-one lead against the Florida Marlins in the National League Championship Series. Josh Beckett stymied the Cubs in Game Five in Florida, and the Cubs imploded in Games Six, which included the infamous Steve Bartman incident, and Game Seven and went home to a stunning series loss.

Sosa was 8-for-26 (.308) with two homers in the NLCS, which would be the final postseason series of his career. There were reports that Kenny Lofton, the center fielder obtained by the Cubs from Pittsburgh for the stretch drive, chastised Sosa over the amount of time he spent in the batting cage at the expense of other hitters. Nothing much came of the story.

The 2004 season was one of controversy, bitterness, and sniping for the Cubs, who collapsed in the final week of the season to fritter away what looked to be a sure wild-card berth. Until the final day of the season, Sosa stayed above the fray, which included players and Baker complaining about media coverage, especially the commentary of TV announcers Chip Caray and Steve Stone. On the final day of the season after the Cubs had been eliminated from postseason contention, Sosa was not in the starting lineup. Sometime during the game, Sosa left the ballpark apparently without the permission of Baker. The next day, the Cubs alerted the media that they had security video evidence of Sosa leaving Wrigley Field during the early innings of the game. The incident greased the skids for Sosa's exit from Chicago, which happened the following February, when he was traded to the Baltimore Orioles.

Kiley reached Sosa by telephone after the final game, and Sosa expressed bitterness toward Baker, who had said he wanted to see Sosa in tip-top shape for the next season. In a story published by the *Chicago Sun-Times*, Kiley quoted Sosa as saying: "I'm tired of being blamed by Dusty Baker for all the failures of this club. I resent the inference that I'm not prepared. I live my life every minute every day to prepare for combat."

So did the blame for the messy exit lie with Sosa or with Baker? "Hard to say," Pannozzo said. "Obviously, what happened in 2003 and how the season ended, and then the clubhouse changed. We lost some good people who were really good people in the clubhouse that sort of knew how to manage differing personalities within that culture and in that space. There wasn't—I'm not going to say lack of leadership—but there was something missing in there that was there before. I think that really had an impact on how people reacted to certain things. It's hard to say. Looking back on it, it seemed like there was a lot of negativity in general. It was just sort of a bad ending to a great story unfortunately. And I don't put the blame on Sammy. Some of it, yes, sure. But not all of it. You can't because there were all sorts of mitigating things going on, circumstances at the time that impacted things going on in that clubhouse."

Kiley echoed much of those sentiments. "Again, it's a he-said, he-said story," he said. "I called him. As I recall, Sammy said the higher-ups, meaning Dusty and maybe the front office, all knew he was leaving early because it was the last day of the season. Then the question was Sammy might have said he left toward one of the later innings. I can't be positive on that. But I think he said he left toward the end [of the game]. Then the Cubs were ready to jump me the next day that they had him pulling out of the parking lot in the second or third inning. That was a totally different story. From that point on, the Cubs were out to cut ties. They were ready to go with Dusty and get rid of Sammy. Those two had butted heads on occasion."

* * *

So what is Sammy Sosa's legacy with the Chicago Cubs? He is the franchise leader in home runs (545) and ranks second in slugging percentage (.569), OPS (.928), third in RBIs (1,414) and intentional walks (140) and fourth in total bases (3,980). He also ranks in the top 10 in many other offensive categories. He also was wildly popular with fans, who cheered his every exploit. Sosa brought people to the ballpark. And once those fans were inside the ballpark, Sosa lifted them up out of the seats and onto their feet.

His messy exit from the Cubs no doubt has hurt that legacy, as have the whispers of steroid use. Sosa testified before Congress in 2005 that he had never taken illegal performance-enhancing drugs. Although fluent in English, Sosa had his representative speak for him, saying he was uncomfortable speaking before Congress in his second language. In 2009 *The*

New York Times reported that Sosa tested positive for PEDs in 2003, further clouding the issue.

The Ricketts family, which purchased the Cubs from the Tribune Co. in 2009, has kept Sosa at arm's length. Chairman Tom Ricketts said at the 2018 Cubs convention: "I really believe that all the players from that era who were in that performance-enhanced era, that steroid era as people call it, I think we owe them a lot of understanding. I think we have to put ourselves in their shoes and be very, very sympathetic to everything, all the decisions they had to make. As it turned out, after testing was begun…a large number of players tested positive. I think we all have to be really, really sensitive and sympathetic in understanding their situation. But I also believe players from that era owe us a little bit of honesty, too. I kind of feel like the only way to turn this page is to just put everything on the table. I think that's kind of a better answer in the long run. We'll see what happens in the future."

We're still waiting for that future. There is a way for Sosa to come back and one that would get Ricketts off the hook. The Cubs have established a team Hall of Fame. The electorate for the Cubs Hall of Fame is made up of former Cubs players who have been elected to the National Baseball Hall of Fame as well as a panel of media members. The group operates independently of Cubs ownership. If Sosa is elected to the Cubs Hall of Fame when his name appears on the ballot, the team will have little choice but to bring him back, at least for an induction ceremony.

Perhaps it would have helped Sosa—both with the Cubs and with Hall of Fame voters—had he embarked on a public relations campaign and said specifically what he had done or not done concerning performance-enhancing drugs. Sosa might have bought himself some goodwill—and maybe more Hall of Fame votes—had he taken this tack.

As far as Sosa's legacy goes, the opinions are varied. "His legacy? A complicated one," said Pat Hughes, the Cubs' radio play-by-play voice since 1996. "He should maybe come clean and say, 'Yes, I know I was never tested positively, and nobody ever proved anything.' But come on. He weighed what 40 pounds more than he did a year or two earlier? He looked like a muscleman compared to an average human being. And it was definitely different. So there was something going on there. I don't know what it was. Also, let me say this: I don't have any knowledge of him taking anything. So maybe I'm out of line even suggesting he should come clean. But I never spent a lot of time in the clubhouse. I usually went in to get the lineups and then I'm out of there. I have my own job to do, and my job is not easy. I don't want to waste your time or mine. That's my approach, and it still is. So I don't know what pills they took."

Chuck Wasserstrom worked with Sharon Pannozzo in media relations for years before moving to baseball operations for the 2004 season. Wasserstrom interviewed Sosa for a blog post in 2017. Sosa professed his innocence. "I feel proud of what I did," he told Wasserstrom. "The only thing is: they can say whatever they want to say about me. First of all, I'm clean. They don't have a case on me. I never failed a drug test. Never in my life."

Interviewed in 2022, Wasserstrom spoke of Sosa's legacy. "I wish his legacy would be what his legacy should be," he said. "I don't think it will ever be there. And I don't know why. In some ways, you do know why. But others have been forgiven. Why he has not been, I don't know. I think a tone was set by people who didn't know him. For whatever reasons, the masses were okay with that. I don't know why revisionist history became more prevalent. It didn't seem to bother people when he was hitting the home runs. And there was no actual proof that he did anything illegal, no matter what you think, other than the corked bat, and what year was that? And what happened in '03? [The Cubs went to the National League Championship Series.] And once he came back [from the corked-bat suspension], they didn't jump off his bandwagon, did they? I wish I could answer that fairly. Even in '98, he didn't exactly burst onto the scene out of nowhere. This is somebody who had close to 40 homers three straight years. It's unfortunate."

For Pannozzo, what Sosa and McGwire did to revive baseball after the 1994 players' strike should not be discounted when it comes to Sosa's legacy. "You look at Sammy in an even bigger picture because I feel that what Sammy and Mark were doing in '98 really was directly responsible for helping to bring baseball back," she said. "People forget how bad it was after '94. It was bad. Fans had lot of anger. The stands weren't full like they were prior to that. I think that MLB, in their infinite wisdom, saw an opportunity that maybe they didn't think of what it was accomplishing. It was big enough event where they felt they wanted to be engaged in, which is why we would have that big press conference in St. Louis. That doesn't happen independently of Major League Baseball. What Sammy and Mark did that year, in my opinion, was sort of galvanize a country, a country around this sort of David and Goliath happening with Sammy and Mark and two really good individuals who are in this season-long, almost, battle. There were people who loved them both. It was this epic battle."

So the multimillion-dollar question remains: should Sosa be a Hall of Famer? The Baseball Writers Association of America said an emphatic no during Sosa's 10 years on the BBWAA ballot. Candidates must get 75 percent of votes cast to gain enshrinement. If a player fails to garner 5 percent, he falls off the ballot. Sosa came nowhere near 75 percent, peaking at 18.5 percent in his final year of eligibility. He nearly fell off the ballot twice, getting 7.2 percent in his second year and 6.6 percent in his third year. McGwire opened at 23.5 percent of the vote in his first year but fell to 12.3 percent in his final year.

Barry Bonds and Roger Clemens, two players also linked to PED use, inched their respective ways up in Hall of Fame balloting but ultimately fell short. Bonds opened at 36.2 percent and finished with 66 percent of the vote. Clemens had 37.6 percent in his first year and 65.2 percent in his final year on the BBWAA ballot. The prevailing opinion among BBWAA voters seemed to be that Bonds and Clemens were closer to being Hall of Famers before whispers of PED use became louder, but that Sosa was not.

All of these players will have a court of second resort in the form of various committees set up by the Hall of Fame. Again, opinion is split among those who were around Sosa. "I can't say yes," Hughes said. "But if somebody like a veterans' committee or if some other committee feels that he is worthy and they vote him in, you would never hear a peep out of me. I would never criticize them and I would say, 'Good for Sammy' because deep down I like Sammy. I even was there in Texas when he hit No. 600 as a Ranger. And I made a point after the game because I liked him. I went down, and he looked at me and said, 'Hey, Pat! How are you?' And he gave me a big bear hug. And I may have been the only Chicago media member that did go down there and see him and congratulate him. I was happy for him. And he was happy that I went into the clubhouse to say, 'Nice going, 600, Sammy! How about that, man?' So yeah, it's tough one."

Cubs broadcaster Ron Coomer also is hesitant to proclaim Sosa a Hall of Famer. "I would say as of right now, no," he said. "There are other people who have done the same thing that aren't in, that I would say no because of what they have done. The cause and effect of some of the things of what they did and affected other people—to me, that's terrible. So I'm a no. I'm a no today. Let's put it that way. I feel like that [steroids] issue in our game has a lot of fingers to it. There's a lot of fault. I played right in that era. I have a lot of opinions on it that we don't need to get into here. But I think there's a lot of blame to go around. And to just pin it on the guys that were playing, they did it okay, great. But there were a whole boatload of people that capitalized on what happened and turned their head to the issue and didn't want to know until it got brought out by another player. I think there's a lot to that whole scenario."

Mike Kiley, the media member most trusted by Sosa and a former BBWAA voter, also replied negatively. "I never voted for him for the Hall of Fame," he said. "It's a long list of people who should be in the Hall of Fame. You put Sammy on the list, and he's down the list from the pitchers and the hitters that most people would put in the Hall of Fame ahead of him. He was a good player, made his impact. He should be happy with it. He really should. I'm sure he still feels he's been put upon and labeled something that he's not. At this point, you gotta get over it and move on and have a good life."

Does Kiley base his opinion on the steroid issue or for other reasons? "I would say no for other reasons," he said. "He had great moments, as we all know. He had great moments, but he had just a good career. Great moments, good career. But there's a lot of players who wish they could say that. I understand those people [who want him in]. It's just sort of a feel when you look at it. I just don't see a whole body of work that's Hall of Fame."

Those who worked for the Cubs and were around Sosa every day say yes. "Yes, that's easy for me," former manager Jim Riggleman said. "I don't care how they do it whether it's Barry Bonds, Sammy, McGwire if they've got to designate some way to put an asterisk on there or put some designation that, 'Here are some things that were happening at that time. Let's not ignore the impact that these guys had on the game.' And we will never know how many people were doing that stuff. We think of it so much as these hitters, but the pitchers were doing it. For me, he should be in. I hate that some guys get in after they pass on. I hope that Sammy and Mark and Barry Bonds get recognized while they're still alive."

Former Cubs front-office executive Wasserstrom concurs that Sosa deserves induction. "To me, yes, because the numbers," he said. "He put up numbers that are deserving of it. Just because somebody doesn't like something doesn't make you the moral judge, which is what we've become. Do I think there are others who aren't in who should be who were 'convicted of something,' and that's the reason why? Well, if your moral compass says, 'You've been convicted of it, then I can't let you in,' I can't tell you what you should be doing and have you listen to me. But he wasn't 'convicted of anything.' He has been guilty until proven innocent. How is he going to prove himself innocent? To me, it's not right. People make the judgments. And at a certain point in time, for what, you feel that good about yourself that you can decide you're the moral compass for all of America? And he wasn't a one-year wonder. You take what he did from that whole span from '95 to 2003, you put that decade up there, stack that up against almost anybody. And he was driving in 100-plus runs, even though people will come up with something, 'Well, RBI is not a real stat, just like batting average isn't a real stat.'"

Pannozzo, perhaps the non-uniformed Cubs person who was closest to Sosa for many years, also thinks he deserves induction. "I do," she said. "I absolutely do because you have to look what's going on. The Hall of Fame has their rules they follow. Again, you look at what's happening in the world and the time that this player was playing. And you look at what everybody else is doing and what are accepted norms. I feel he was singled out with a group of other people at something that was widely accepted and overlooked, however you want to term it. There was a lot going on that nobody wanted to address. He has the numbers. His contributions should be acknowledged in the bigger scope of what was going on during the course of his career. And the fact is, you have to give him and Mark McGwire credit for what happened in '98 in helping to bring back the game because the game was suffering badly. Anybody who lived day-to-day, 162 games, back then, it was rough for a few years. And Sammy and Mark helped to turn that around—in a big way, in a big, spectacular way."

4

The Phenom:
Kerry Wood

IF THE WORD "PHENOM" ISN'T UNIQUE TO BASEBALL, IT COMES
pretty close. The word conjures up images of some raw-boned,
flaxen-haired farm boy throwing the ball 100 miles per hour
and leaving batters shaking their heads as they trudge back to
the dugout with bats on their shoulders.

Or a phenom could be some whippet-quick outfielder with
an equally quick bat, the "five-tool" kid who gets fans talking all
over again about Willie Mays or Roberto Clemente. In baseball
parlance a phenom is the youngster who appears on the scene like
a flash and all but guarantees a world championship for his team
and a spot in Cooperstown for himself when his career is all over.

"Phenom" is short for "phenomenon." Kerry Wood was
both phenom and phenomenon with the Chicago Cubs. Wood

eventually grew out of the phenom stage with age, but the phenomenon of Wood never went away—not through myriad injuries, team disappointments, or even Wood signing with the Cleveland Indians after the 2008 season. He eventually was traded to the New York Yankees, where he shared a bullpen with Mariano Rivera.

Wood returned to the Cubs for the 2011 season, and there was some doubt he would return for 2012. But during the opening ceremonies of the 2012 Cubs fan convention in January, the team's radio announcer, Pat Hughes, told fans he "had some breaking news," that Wood had signed a free-agent deal to stay with the Cubs. The crowd that was packed into the hotel ballroom ate it up. By May, Wood decided that he had had enough and announced his retirement. Wood's final appearance came on May 18 in a game against the Chicago White Sox at Wrigley Field. He struck out the only batter he faced, Dayan Viciedo, in the eighth inning and walked off the field to a loud ovation while being embraced on the field by his son.

The circle was complete, and despite not living up to the wild expectations of others and perhaps even the more tempered expectations he had for himself, Wood will be remembered forever as an all-time beloved Cub. "He's got to go down as one of the all-time great Cubs," said Jim Riggleman, Wood's manager when the phenomenon was born in 1998. "The guys who were long before me, Gabby Hartnett and the guys I grew up watching—Billy Williams and Ernie Banks and Ron Santo and that crew there—then you get into Grace and Sosa and Sandberg era. Then you get into the Kerry Wood and Mark Prior and Rod Beck and some of the great performances. But for me, he should be remembered for being a great Cub, a guy that left it all out there for you. When he was out there, he was max-effort and he was doing everything he could to go deep into a game. Just a total pleasure. He was a team guy. Just nothing but positive stuff. But certainly, he's got to be one of the great Cubs of all time."

Wood came up to the Cubs as a shy, fresh-faced right-hander in April of 1998 after dazzling teammates in spring training with his blazing fastball and wicked breaking pitches.

After one Cactus League start against the Milwaukee Brewers, Bruce Miles asked catcher Scott Servais where Wood ranked just in terms of stuff among the pitchers he had caught over his major league career up until then.

Servais didn't utter a word. He simply held up his index finger: No. 1. He also agreed with his manager's assessment of where Wood ranks in the pantheon of Cubs. "His legacy is one of the greatest pitchers the Cubs have ever had," he said in 2018. "There's no question for me. Where the Cubs were at that point, where the franchise was, there had been a lot of losing seasons. The '98 team, we got into the wild-card, created an excitement. He was a big part of that. It was something the fans could grasp on to. When Greg Maddux left, Kerry Wood was the next guy. The franchise definitely needed that guy."

The Cubs took Wood in the first round of the 1995 amateur draft, using the fourth overall pick to select the rawboned right-hander out of Grand Prairie High School in Texas. He drew comparisons to another Texan hurler—Roger Clemens. At the time, Cubs scouting director Al Goldis said: "We got the best pitcher in the draft, maybe the best player in the draft. I haven't seen a guy throw like this in 10 years." Goldis went so far as to say he would have taken Wood over Dwight "Doc" Gooden if they were both in the same draft.

Wood shot his way up the Cubs' minor leagues. He led the organization's entire farm system in strikeouts in 1996 with 136 in 114 ⅓ innings. Wood went 10–2 with a 2.91 ERA that year.

The meteoric rise continued. Just shy of his 21st birthday in the spring of 1998, he made a quick impression on his teammates in Arizona. To a man, they wanted Wood to break camp with the big club and open the season with the team in Miami.

But it was not to be, and unlike 2015, when talk of "service-time manipulation" was rampant surrounding another phenom, Kris Bryant, there was no such talk in March of 1998, when the Cubs opened the regular season. "To be honest with you, I don't remember any discussion about it," Riggleman said. "Kerry had a great spring. There was just a general feeling that he was so young and hadn't pitched that much in the minor leagues, and, 'Let's just let him start down there in the minor leagues and see where he's at.' Kerry had one game in the minor leagues [in 1998] and went five innings and struck out 11. So it was probably going to happen pretty quickly."

Wood's call-up came April 12 after left-handed relief pitcher Bob Patterson suffered an injury on a fielding play. The Cubs decided to move veteran lefty Terry Mulholland from the starting rotation and promote Wood to join a staff that featured Kevin Tapani, Mark Clark, Steve Trachsel, and Geremi Gonzalez. Mulholland initially was not happy with his move to the bullpen, but he became one of the Cubs' most valuable and versatile pitchers on their run to the wild-card.

On Easter Sunday 1998, Wood made his major league debut at Olympic Stadium in Montreal. He struck out Mark Grudzielanek, the first batter he faced. Wood wound up pitching four-and-two-thirds innings, giving up four hits and four runs while walking three and striking out seven in a 4–1 Cubs loss to the Montreal Expos. Wood was 2–2 with a 5.89 ERA when he made his fifth major league start against the Houston Astros at Wrigley Field on May 6, a dank, dreary day that attracted only 15,758 fans to the ballpark.

Wood's first pitch of the game hit home-plate umpire Jerry Meals in his facemask. Perhaps that was a reflection of how Wood said he felt warming up in the bullpen before the game. "I don't think I threw any strikes warming up," he said. "I was all over the place. Balls were all over the place, and I think I actually shut it down early and flipped the ball to [pitching coach] Phil Regan and said, 'We're done. I'm loose. It's only going to get worse. Let's go.' It was ugly warming up. I know that."

When the afternoon ended, Wood had struck out 20 batters of a potent Houston lineup that included future Hall of Famers Craig Biggio and Jeff Bagwell. The Astros went on to win the National League Central with a record of 102–60, finishing 12 ½ games over the Cubs (90–73), who needed a 163rd game to win the wild-card. Houston's 3-4-5 hitters—Bagwell, Jack Howell, and Moises Alou—went a combined 0-for-9 all on strikeouts. If you're looking for a moment when a phenomenon was born, it was when Wood struck out Derek Bell to end the game, giving a little fist pump as he did. The Cubs won the game 2–0, and Wood gave up one hit and walked no one. In 55 minor league games before his major league debut, Wood never once tossed a complete game, and the 20-strikeout game was his only complete game of the 1998 season.

The phenomenon continues to this day, even though Wood missed the entire 1999 season because of Tommy John surgery and through various injuries and illnesses over the years. "I think it all boils down to the 20-strikeout game, I really do," Hughes said in 2022. "It just came out of the blue. We needed some good news. It was right after Harry Caray passed in spring training in February. It came on the heels of a hideous 1997 season in which we were 0–14 and done by the middle of April. This was still early in the '98 season, the first week of May, and we *needed* some good news. Everyone was kind of down. The team was playing decent ball, nothing fantastic. But he just stunned the baseball world with his 20 strikeouts. Here was a guy making his fifth big league start, 20 years old. And he had never even pitched a complete game in the minor leagues...he sets an all-time National League record for strikeouts in a game and ties Clemens with the all-time record."

Wood gave up only one hit in the game, a single to future Cubs infielder Ricky Gutierrez in the third inning, when Gutierrez's grounder barely skittered past the outstretched glove of Cubs third baseman Kevin Orie. The official scorer immediately ruled the ball a hit, and little was said about the call on the Cubs' telecast. Wood agreed with call. When Gutierrez joined the Cubs in 2000, he walked past a TV set that was showing a replay of the game one day during spring training. Without breaking stride, Gutierrez looked up and said, "I got a hit off that sorry..."

Managing in the minor leagues in 2018, Gutierrez gave all credit to Wood on the eve of the 20th anniversary of the game. "We were just like, 'Wow, we're witnessing something special,'" he said. "We're still up there trying to grind, and it got to a point where we were just trying to make contact, just get a hit, just put the ball in play. He was just mowing us down left and right. When I first got the hit, it went off [Orie's] glove to his left, off the tip of his glove, and everybody pretty much thought it was a hit. I thought it was a hit. I didn't even look to the scoreboard. Once I did look up, it was flashed up right off the bat. There was no hesitation by the scorekeeper. Later on, down the road during the game, there were going to be questions with it."

None of those questions came from Wood. "Base hit all the time," he said. "I would never tell Ricky that. I tell Ricky it's an error every time. No, it was a base hit. It never crossed my mind. It really never did. Even if that was in the fifth inning, I don't think it would have crossed my mind because the only way Kevin gets to the ball is if he lays out and dives. And at that point, Ricky still had decent wheels, and you're not going to get him on a slow-hit ball where you got to leave your feet. It nicked his glove, but he was in full stride, full stretch, full everything. But, no, it was a base hit all the way."

Wood and that day's official scorer, Don Friske, struck up a friendly conversation in the press box in 2017. "Everyone has an opinion on scoring and everything else," Friske said. "I don't know if it made me feel good. It made me feel good just to hear the person who was involved in it say it."

And who knows? If Wood had taken no-hitter into the late innings, would it have affected his approach on the mound? Would he have overthrown the ball, lost his control, and be forced out of the game? We'll never know.

The 20-strikeout performance was so dominant that it drew comparisons in the postgame excitement to baseball's best. "I've never seen anything like this," said Ron Santo, the Hall of Fame Cubs third baseman who was working as a radio broadcaster for the Cubs. "You know what? I think you might see it from him again. That's how good this kid is. I'm not trying to put pressure on him. It's obvious. The only thing comparable was Sandy Koufax's no-hitter when he pitched a perfect game against us at Dodger Stadium. Joe Amalfitano struck out for the second out of the ninth inning, and Harvey Kuenn was next. Joey stopped Harvey and said, 'No, you shouldn't go up there.' I've never seen anything like this.'"

Even Wood's teammates were in awe. "It's definitely a gift you don't see very often," said first baseman Mark Grace after the game. "I've never seen it. There's Nolan Ryan. I've never seen Roger Clemens other than on TV. In this day and age, when offense is so unbelievably out of control, you've got a guy like him who can just absolutely overmatch the best hitters in the game. There's nobody even close to throwing as hard as he does. He's not even airing it out yet. He's ready to go, but he's not putting that extra something into it. He's one of those guys who can cruise anywhere from 93 to 96. Now he gets into a pinch, and you're going to have to hit something 99–100. Doc Gooden used to be that. Doc used to cruise at 91, 93–94. Then you have to go up to 96–97 with him. But Woody's got more than Doc in his heyday."

Wood's pitching coach, Regan, was a teammate of Koufax. Not given to exaggeration, Regan was left marveling at his protégé's performance. "You don't teach that kind of an arm; it's there," Regan said. "He has a nice easy delivery. Smooth. The fastball jumps, and they can't react to it. I was with Koufax, and he was a dominating pitcher. I don't think he was any more dominating than this kid was today."

Is it any wonder a phenomenon was born? The day after the 20-strikeout game, the Cubs and Wood held a news conference fittingly enough in a room next to Gate K at Wrigley Field. The modest Wood turned down various requests to appear on TV shows, but he drew a crowd of media wherever the Cubs went from there.

In his start after the 20-strikeout game, Wood struck out 13 in seven innings against the expansion Arizona Diamondbacks in Phoenix in front of many snowbirding Cubs fans. Six days later, the nascent Wood phenomenon took another strange twist, when he struck out *only* eight in six innings at Cincinnati. It turns out Wood had gashed a finger on his pitching hand. "I cut my finger [on a soda can] a couple of days ago," he revealed after the game. "I had to put Super Glue on it to keep it shut, and [the glue] came off."

That victory was Wood's fourth in a row, and it ran his record to 5–2 and lowered his ERA to 2.90. There was no stopping the phenomenon after that. "Kerry was very good," Riggleman said after the Cincinnati Reds game. "We're in a situation where we're getting spoiled a little bit. We expect him to be great every time. Today he was very good. We'll certainly take that."

Perhaps the most interesting aspect of the Wood phenomenon in 1998 was that it took place during the summer when the Cubs' Sammy Sosa and the St. Louis Cardinals' Mark McGwire took part in their historic home run duel. Both shattered Roger Maris' single-season home run record of 61. Chicks may have dug the long ball, as the Nike ad claimed, but everybody, it seems, also wanted to come out and see a power pitcher throw blue-flame heat. "Everyone wanted to know, 'Could he do it again?'" Hughes said. "I sometimes wonder, and there's no way of knowing. It's one of those unanswerable things, but had he not struck out 20 in a game, how would his career maybe have been different? I'll tell you why I say that. He would have games where he would strike out 11 or 13, which is still a tremendous number in a big league game, and the fans would think, *Eh, only 13?* I felt like saying, 'You can't expect 20 strikeouts every game. You can't even expect 14 or 15. Ten is a lot to expect every single game.' But I don't think a lot of fans understood that. I think they expected him to do it again, and obviously, he never even came close, which does not surprise me."

Wood's demeanor remained low-key during the summer of '98, as it did for most of his career. His relationship with the media was mostly cordial; he bristled only when he felt reporters were harping on an injury or asking about his pitching mechanics, which often were criticized for being stressful on his arm. "On the days he pitched, he knew what he had to do," said Chuck Wasserstrom, who worked in the Cubs' media relations department in 1998 before later moving to baseball operations. "He understood that there were responsibilities. He came in young, and we were able to kind of work with him so he didn't come in jaded. He didn't come in with any negative connotations about anything. The only work with him was to clue him in on what people might be trying to talk about, and you did that with anybody. He was very easy to work with on that. I don't recall any incidents where he wasn't accommodating."

Riggleman agreed that Wood handled the acclaim. "Extremely well," he said. "He was really low-key. Some of the veteran guys, Grace in particular, kind of took him under his wing. The veteran pitchers on the team, nobody was envious, jealous, or anything like that. Everybody was really behind him because he had a great personality. He was quiet. He had a quiet confidence about himself. His teammates respected that. On the planes there was a lot of card playing going on in those days. He jumped right in there and was playing cards with the big boys. He handled it very well. I think he realized that, *This is hard up here, man. I'm doing pretty good. This is hard. I gotta keep working at this.*"

For Wood it was all new to him, and he was somewhat bemused by it. "I had hype coming out of high school, so I was used to some of the media attention but not on a national scale like what was getting ready to happen after that game," he said. "Everything I did became really important, which was really weird for me at the time. I was just a private guy. I just wanted to come to work and just play baseball. I don't think anybody expected, me included, five starts into it that things like that were going to happen. But it raised the bar for me personally. At 20 years old, I thought I could go out and do that every time. I expected to go out the next time and go, 'That was fun. I should do that every time.'"

The Cubs shut Wood down in September of 1998 because of elbow soreness, a foreshadowing of things to come the next spring, when Wood finally blew out the elbow. Wood did come back to pitch in Game Three of the 1998 National League Division Series at Wrigley Field against the Atlanta Braves, but his elbow was a ticking time bomb.

In 2022 Riggleman addressed the issue and how he used Wood. "Kerry has been very kind to me when that question has been asked," he said. "On the 10- and 20-year anniversary [of the 20-strikeout game], somebody called me. I guess they called everybody who had managed Kerry and asked me the question, 'Do you think you pitched him too much?'

"I said, 'You know, we probably did.' We didn't know it at the time, but looking back on it, if I had it to do over, I probably would have pitched him less. Some of the other people who were asked that question basically said, 'No, I don't think I pitched him too much. It is what it is.' I think because I did take a little accountability for it, the guy who was asking the questions appreciated that. What I was doing, I was trying to hold myself accountable. But in reality I don't think we pitched him too much. It seems like everybody who has this type of velocity and the power and the torque that they're dealing with, it seems like they do get hurt. When we drafted him, I didn't think about it at the time, but I do remember somebody said, 'Yeah, when we drafted him, we knew he had a questionable elbow.' But he dominated the state of Texas, so we took him. We were hoping that he holds up. If we had pitched him less, he probably would have held up longer. Basically, if I had it to do over, selfishly to protect myself, I would have pitched him less so I would not have been criticized about using him the way we did."

In fact, Riggleman said he was criticized for the opposite reason. "I've told this many times," he said. "Nobody ever in '98 was critical of me for pitching him. What I was criticized for was taking him out. There were some 13-strikeout games, 12 and 13 in six and seven innings, and I would take him out, and the fans would be howling because they want to see more. 'So he's got 115 pitches. He's good.' But to protect myself, I probably would have pitched him less. In today's world, he would be pitching five innings at most, maybe six."

The elbow finally gave out in the spring of 1999. During a Cactus League game against the Anaheim Angels in Tempe, Arizona, Wood threw a warmup pitch that went over the catcher's head and to the backstop. No one really noticed it, and Wood went on to finish his start. As is the custom during spring training games, reporters are permitted into the locker room to interview the day's starting pitcher while the game is going on. Wood greeted reporters and gave no indication something was wrong.

But the next day, word came out that Wood had hurt his right elbow and that he would be sent for further examination. The verdict was that Wood would need reconstructive Tommy John surgery on the elbow and that he would miss the entire 1999 season. Wood was crestfallen, as were his teammates. The Cubs missed Wood during the season. After they got off to a promising 32–23 start, they completely fell apart, finishing 67–95, costing Riggleman and pitching coach Marty DeMerritt their jobs.

Wood came back in 2000 and went 8–7 with 4.80 ERA, making 23 starts after beginning the season on a minor league rehab assignment. In 2001 and 2002, Wood was solid, going

12–6 and 12–11, respectively, and striking out more batters than innings pitched in each season. The fastball was still good, and Wood had abandoned the slurve pitch that put so much stress on his elbow.

A seasoned veteran, Wood enjoyed his best season in 2003, going 14–11 with a 3.20 ERA as the Cubs won the National League Central under manager Dusty Baker. In the divisional series against the Braves, Wood went 2–0 with a 1.76 ERA. In the final game of the best-of-five series at Turner Field, Wood pitched eight innings in a 5–1 victory. After the game Wood and some of his teammates sprayed champagne on Cubs fans who made the trek down to Atlanta.

In the National League Championship Series against the Florida Marlins, Wood turned in a quality start in Game Three and got a no-decision in a 5–4 victory in 11 innings. The Cubs took a 3–1 series lead but were shut down in Game Five by Josh Beckett in a dominant performance. With two chances to win the NLCS and advance to their first World Series since 1945, the Cubs had young aces Mark Prior and Wood ready to go. The Game Six collapse, when the Marlins scored eight runs in the eighth inning of the "Bartman Game," shook the life out of the Cubs, but they still had a chance to win in Game Seven.

Wood started but gave up three runs in the first inning. He helped himself and the Cubs with a two-run homer in the bottom of the second, when the Cubs tied the game. The Cubs went ahead 5–3 in the third, sending the nervous Wrigley Field crowd—and those on the streets outside the ballpark—into a frenzy. But Wood and the Cubs couldn't hold the lead as he gave up seven runs in five-and-two-thirds innings, and the Marlins came away with a 9–6 victory, extending the Cubs' heartbreak in stunning fashion. Wood did not hold back on himself after the game. "I choked," he said flatly as he answered questions from reporters in the Cubs clubhouse.

A triceps strain limited Wood to 22 starts in 2004. Shoulder problems derailed Wood's seasons in 2005 and 2006 after he underwent surgery on August 31, 2005. He pitched in only four games in '06. The Cubs returned to the postseason in 2007 for the first time in four years, and Wood pitched as a reliever in 22 regular-season games and two postseason games, when the Cubs were swept in three games by the Arizona Diamondbacks.

Wood's rotation mates in the early 2000s included the likes of Carlos Zambrano, Matt Clement, and Prior, another highly touted phenom and first-round draft pick. Like Wood, Prior suffered a number of injuries, which shortened his career to just five years (2002–06). Wood and Prior often were lumped together in conversation as talented pitchers who were oft-injured. Wood understood, but in 2007 he told Jeff Vorva of the *Daily Southtown* that it was more complicated than that. "We're good friends, and I talk to him quite a bit," Wood told Vorva. "As far as us being lumped together—that's completely out of our control. That's what's written and said on TV. We have similar paths. I saw him a couple of weekends ago, and he seemed in good spirits. I don't know how far he is in his rehab. He says it's going well. He definitely has some hard work ahead of him. But he has the makeup to get it done."

Wood made a successful transformation to closer in 2008, saving 34 games and looking comfortable in his new role. Pitchers John Smoltz and Cubs teammate Ryan Dempster also made the transition from starter to closer. (Dempster went back to being a starting pitcher near the end of his career.) "It doesn't surprise me," said Ron Coomer, a teammate of Wood's in 2001 and the Cubs' current radio analyst. "First of all, Kerry is a great athlete. You play golf with him, he's a very good athlete. But it made sense to me. If a guy is breaking down a little bit with a body part, instead of running him out there as starter and tearing him down with 100-plus pitches, he can close, and his body can recover faster. It fits. And he's got the stuff for it. He was throwing 97-98 miles an hour with a great curveball. So it made sense."

With the Cubs in a cost-cutting mode after the 2008 season, Wood signed a two-year deal with the Cleveland Indians, for whom he saved 20 games in 2009. He was dealt to the Yankees at the July 31 trading deadline in 2010. He got into three games of the American League Division Series against the Minnesota Twins and four games of the ALCS against the Texas Rangers. The Cubs brought Wood home in 2011, and he worked in 55 games. He was a free agent after the season, when Theo Epstein took over as team president. Epstein and Wood reached agreement at the convention, but Wood didn't have much left in the tank and he appeared in just 10 games.

Wood went out to a standing ovation after he struck out Viciedo on his final day as major leaguer. He went out with no second thoughts or regrets. "It was time," he said. "You saw how things were going. I couldn't bounce back. I couldn't recover. I couldn't do my job. It was time. I was making it difficult for the other guys in the pen. It was unfair."

For his career Wood was 86–75 with a 3.67 ERA, 63 saves, and 1,582 strikeouts in 1,380 innings pitched. His 10.3 strikeouts per nine innings rank him ninth all time in Major League Baseball history. In the pantheon of Cubs pitchers, Wood ranks third in hits per nine innings, strikeouts per nine innings, and total strikeouts. His 12.6 strikeouts per nine innings in his Rookie of the Year season in 1998 ranks first in team history.

Wood remained in the Cubs organization after retirement. He and his wife, Sarah, are active in community and charitable events. The fact that Wood, a Texas kid, took so naturally to Chicago is another reason for his enduring popularity since the 20-strikeout game. "There's a lot of factors: young kid, nice kid, really nice kid," Coomer said. "Good teammate. Everybody likes him. Now all of a sudden you have this extreme success and you can understand why this city put their arms round him and said, 'That's our guy.' And you can understand that. That's how Chicago is. If you're good people, they're going to find out quick. And when you can perform the way he did, it's good."

For Wasserstrom, Wood's youth and the fact that he was power pitcher played into the phenomenon. "He was so young when he came up," he said. "Remember he was 20 years old. When you talk about phenoms, it's kind of tough for somebody to have that label stick with them when they come up at 24 or 25 years old. But as a 20 year old, he had some pretty extraordinary success early on, and if you get that early modicum of success right away with Cubs fans, that will carry it through. You kind of have blinders on if there is a down year or two because of the success you've already had. They don't turn on you. That first year, beyond the 20-strikeout year, he went to the playoffs. He got shut down for September but came back and had a creditable start in the postseason. After the injuries he came back and had a solid 2003, a playoff year. In those big years, he was a major part of it. Power pitchers are always going to get that built-in buzz anyway. And the baby face. Because as young as he was, that kind of stuck there, too."

For research historian Ed Hartig, the phenomenon of Kerry Wood is steeped in something deeper than the 20-strikeout game. "There's no doubt that the 20-strikeout game was a lot of it," he said. "With Wood it even goes before that. I think Cub fans were desperate for a homegrown pitcher. A couple years before, we had Lance Dickson, who kind of burned out. Maddux never had this kind of hype. Dennis Lamp, Mike Krukow, Frank Castillo, Steve Trachsel, Ray Burris maybe had a little bit. That was the wrong reason. I think Burris got lumped in as the next Fergie Jenkins. The Cubs really hadn't had a stud pitcher in a long, long time. And not only that, he was Texas. He was this farm boy. We heard the stories of him throwing 175 pitches in a high school game. And he's hitting 95 to 100. I think he was the exception to everything. He had a good start to spring training [in 1998]. He got sent down. Terry Collins of the Angels commented that if the Cubs are sending Kerry Wood down, he's putting all this money on the Cubs to win the World Series because they've got the greatest rotation in all of baseball... People were kind of starved for that type [of pitcher]. Then he has the 20-strikeout game. You watch him being interviewed, and he's a kid. He's a baby. His hands are shaking. He doesn't know about the strikeouts. He's more happy that he didn't walk guys. I think it was the timing and the fact that fans were desperate for someone like that they could root for."

Given the benefit of time, Wood seems to have his career—the ups, the downs, the elation, the disappointments—in perspective. One thing he says he doesn't do is let that one day in May of 1998 define his life or his career—even if it did kick off a phenomenon. "You don't ever want to be defined, especially when you have a long career, by one game," he said in 2018. "But it most certainly put me on the map. People, when they remember me being a strikeout guy, that's what they're going to remember. I feel like I had several more meaningful games, more important games [that] in my mind were better games because they were team wins and not just a single performance in the first part of May in a meaningless game at the time. So

I look back on it with great memories and, as every year rolls around, I see the highlights again. It showed me that personally that I belong here. It's not a fluke that I'm here. I deserve to be here. I can compete at this level. Then again, it set the bar for the rest of my career, the rest of my outings after that. You can look at my career any way you want. You could look at it as it was a disappointment—I didn't achieve what I was supposed to achieve. Or you can look at it as I battled adversity and came back and grinded through and got 14 years out of a career that a lot of people and doctors said I wasn't going to."

PART 2

THE MANAGERS

WHEN DUSTY BAKER ARRIVED IN CHICAGO, HE HAD TO tamp down expectations. "My name is Dusty, not Messiah," Johnnie B. Baker said during his introductory news conference in November 2002. Baker then proceeded to hand out T-shirts with "Why Not Us?" printed across the front. A Chicago Cubs higher-up thought the sentiment was unbecoming of franchise with the history of the Cubs (although history at that point suggested it was quite becoming), and those T-shirts weren't seen again.

When Lou Piniella hit town, a sore subject among fans and the burgeoning analytical community was the Cubs' poor on-base percentage, the importance of which was pooh-poohed by Baker, who famously or infamously intoned that walks can "clog the bases." Piniella had a plan. He joked during his opening news conference that he was going to send nine midgets to the plate and have them walk. The Cubs' staff and Piniella himself asked that reporters not emphasize that off-the-cuff remark out of sensitivity.

When Joe Maddon held his first Chicago presser—at the Cubby Bear Lounge kitty corner from Wrigley Field—he offered to buy media members shots and beers. In a bygone time, reporters quickly would have taken Maddon up on the offer. With modern-day editors, publishers, and news and sports directors frowning on such practices during working hours, perhaps only a handful of media members tossed back that shot and beer.

Baker, Piniella, and Maddon are three of the most colorful big-name managers in the history of the Cubs. Their tenure spanned the 2003–2019 seasons—with some notably lesser lights filling the in-between gaps. Any baseball beat reporter would gladly say that if you got to cover Dusty, Lou, and Joe, you would have felt you had died and gone to writer/reporter heaven. Not only are Baker, Piniella, and Maddon three of the most big-name, colorful, and interesting managers in Cubs history, but they're three of the most colorful and quotable managers in all of baseball history.

The Cubs have employed many big-name managers, dating to their beginning as the White Stockings in 1876. Albert Spalding, he of the Spalding Guide and sporting goods, was the team's first official manager. Cap Anson, who leaves behind a complicated legacy in baseball's early efforts to keep the game all-White, is the franchise's all-time winningest manager. Frank Chance, known as "The Peerless Leader," was a player/manager for pennant-winners from 1906 to 1908. He had the distinction of being the last manager before Maddon to win a World Series as manager of the Cubs, when he did so in 1908. He also was the first baseman of the Cubs' celebrated Tinker-to-Evers-to-Chance double-play combination.

Joe McCarthy, Rogers Hornsby, Charlie Grimm, and Gabby Hartnett piloted the Cubs to pennants in the years spanning 1929–45. After a disastrous dalliance with a revolving-door of coaches in the early 1960s, the Cubs hired the volatile Leo Durocher before the 1966 season. During his introduction to Chicago, Durocher said the Cubs were not an eighth-place ballclub. He was right. They finished 10th in his first season in 1966. Durocher's claim to fame was getting the Cubs oh-so-close to the postseason in 1969 before a monumental collapse in September. Known for the not-entirely-accurate quote of, "Nice guys finish last," Durocher was certainly a big name and colorful, but he wasn't such a nice guy, as he feuded with iconic broadcaster Jack Brickhouse and the Chicago press corps all while riding hard on Mr. Cub, Ernie Banks.

Don Zimmer's sometimes unconventional methods won the Cubs a division in 1989. The Cubs thought they had their next big-name winner after firing the self-described "vanilla" Jim Riggleman ("Gentleman Jim," as he was known to those covering him) after the 1999 season. Don Baylor, though a big name from his days as a hard-nosed player, was low-key as a person and he lasted just two-and-a-half years, setting the stage for Baker's grand entrance a few months later.

In the era of big media, Baker, Piniella, and Maddon seemed perfect fits for the spotlight of Chicago and for handling the pressure of a job that carried the weight of history with it. Each had his moments, but only Maddon ultimately succeeded, and even he had his fierce critics. He was shown the door after five years.

5

In Dusty We Trusty

WHEN CHICAGO CUBS PRESIDENT AND GENERAL MANAGER Andy MacPhail decided to fire Don Baylor on the Fourth of July in 2002, he also decided to turn over the GM duties to his assistant Jim Hendry, who previously served as the organization's director of scouting and player development. Hendry reached down to the Cubs' Class Triple A Iowa affiliate and appointed former journeyman catcher Bruce Kimm as interim manager. Meanwhile, out in San Francisco, Dusty Baker was on his way to leading the San Francisco Giants to a World Series in his 10th year as manager after gaining playing fame with the Giants hated rivals, the Los Angeles Dodgers.

Kimm finished the 2002 Cubs season with a record of 33–45. While Baker was considered a "players manager," Kimm was losing the clubhouse and angering his bosses. He was reluctant to play young first-base prospect Hee-Seop Choi despite orders to do so from above. Instead, Kimm stuck with Fred McGriff, saying he wanted to respect the veteran.

In a memorable clubhouse tirade after a tough Sunday night loss in St. Louis on September 8, Kimm burned his final bridge by tearing into his players. Reporters standing outside the clubhouse door heard it all—loudly and clearly. And they wrote it all down in their notepads and reported it. "The way we play the game is bullshit!" Kimm screamed. "If you don't want to do it right, get out of here. It's a damn shame!"

Meanwhile, on the West Coast, Baker was going to the postseason, one that would prove controversial and raise an early red flag to Cubs fans about his managerial style. The Giants were up three games to two against the Anaheim Angels in the World Series after a rousing 16–4 victory at home in Game Five. With two chances to win a world championship, the Giants lost both games in Southern California, and Baker drew criticism for the handling of his pitching staff, a charge that would dog him throughout his managerial career. A rift between Baker and Giants owner Peter Magowan became irreparable, and Baker's contract was not renewed.

In Chicago, Hendry waited patiently. Baker was his guy all along, even though he would have done just fine if he had hired Bob Melvin after what seemed to be a good job interview in the fall. Baker's hiring was met with overall enthusiasm in Chicago. For Hendry, Baker was a big name with a winning pedigree who would bring instant credibility to the dugout and win over his troops. He did that. As proof players sported T-shirts with "In Dusty We Trusty" across the front.

A survivor of prostate cancer, Baker began each morning in his spring training office by flipping on a blender to make a smoothie with ingredients such as bee pollen and honey. Baker even granted Bruce Miles' request to sample the concoction.

Although the smoothie wasn't bad, Miles didn't ask for seconds. On the desk in Baker's office, there was an array of books for players to sample in a kind of Dusty Baker Lending Library. For as well-read as he is, Baker is decidedly old school when it comes to his managing. When pressed during spring training about the importance of on-base percentage, Baker asked if the New York Yankees talked about on-base percentage. Answer: maybe not, but they sure executed it well. Baker's comments about the importance of batters taking walks was widely mocked. He said that sometimes, "walks clog the bases," as if slower players were walking and moving only station to station when subsequent batters got hits. A fanbase that was growing in sophistication about sabermetrics had a field day with that one on various blogs and message boards that were emerging in those days.

The Cubs opened the regular season in New York to play the Mets in an unrelenting April chill. Spotting a couple of beat writers in the bar of the Grand Hyatt hotel while nursing a glass of Scotch, Baker told them: "You better get your boots on because you're going to go through so much shit. And I'm not losing. I...am...not...losing."

Baker peaked too soon in Chicago—both in terms of popularity and on-the-field success.

In the Cubs' ancient rivalry with the St. Louis Cardinals and longtime managerial nemesis Tony La Russa, Baker seemed to get the upper hand during a heated five-game series to start September 2003. Baker responded to criticism by Cardinals pitcher Matt Morris by saying that the Redbirds had a "whole decade of us coming."

When the Cubs clinched their first postseason series victory since 1945 by beating the Braves in Atlanta, the clubhouse at Turner Field was a haze of cigar smoke and champagne spray, and Baker soaked up the well-deserved plaudits. Nothing looked like it was stopping the Cubs—not even the wild-card winning Florida Marlins, who went down three games to one in the National League Championship Series. The Cubs losing Game Five to fireballer Josh Beckett in Miami seemed only to be the equivalent of a stubbed toe. After all, the Cubs were coming home for Games Six and Seven if needed.

What could possibly go wrong?

We all know what happened. The infamous Bartman Game—in which Mark Prior and the Cubs held a 3–0 lead with five outs to go only to see the Marlins score eight runs in the eighth inning—shocked Cubs fans and seared their collective psyche until the Cubs finally won the World Series in 2016. But many never forgave Baker for not coming out to settle down Prior after fan Steve Bartman impeded left fielder Moises Alou's attempt to catch a foul ball. (Fan interference was not called because Alou reached over the wall and into the stands.) It also might have helped if shortstop Alex Gonzalez had not made an error on a bouncing hit right to him during that inning.

But even before that game, Baker raised many eyebrows for allowing Prior to pitch seven innings of a 12–3 blowout win in Game Two. Whatever the case, there was a Game Seven to be won.

The Cubs had Prior's co-ace, Kerry Wood, going in Game Seven, but not even a Wood home run could save them, as the Marlins completed the comeback and went on to win the World Series against the Yankees. To a man the Cubs rued the lost opportunity because they were confident they could beat New York if they had only gotten that far.

The Cubs never got back to the postseason under Baker, whose popularity in Chicago declined with each passing season. The 2004 club won 89 games, one more than the 2003 squad. Baker had more talent at his disposal in '04. Hendry obtained star third baseman Aramis Ramirez in a steal of a trade with the Pittsburgh Pirates during the 2003 season. In the 2003–04 offseason, Hendry made another shrewd trade, sending Choi to the Marlins for first baseman Derrek Lee. And just as spring training was about to begin, Hendry brought pitcher Greg Maddux "home" to Chicago, righting a perceived wrong when previous management allowed Maddux to sign with the Braves after the 1992 season.

But something was not right about the 2004 club. Baker always seemed to thrive on an us-against-them attitude, whether "them" was the media or skeptical or downright abusive fans. During the 2004 season, Baker was more than willing—and justified—to tell of racist hate mail he got from fans upset about the postseason failure of 2003. Things got off to a testy start in spring training of 2004, when everyman closer Joe Borowski (whom the Cubs had plucked out of obscurity in Mexico in 2002) took umbrage at media reports that he was hurt. Borowski indeed was hurt, and Baker turned the closer's reins over to veteran LaTroy Hawkins, a native of nearby Gary, Indiana, and another of Hendry's offseason acquisitions. Upon being named closer early in the regular season, Hawkins called a news conference to announce he wasn't going to talk to the media, adding the kicker that he could do the job of media members but that they couldn't do his job. Needless to say, some media members had a field day with that one, some saying they could blow saves just as well as Hawkins could.

As the season wore on, players and coaches took offense at criticism by team TV broadcasters Chip Caray and Steve Stone. Baker cut short a late-season postgame interview with the duo. The Cubs seemed poised to win the National League wild-card, but a final week collapse saw the Cubs lose seven of their last nine games, including five in a row. Baker and the players seemed distracted, and on the final day of the season, superstar right fielder Sammy Sosa left the ballpark during the game, seemingly without Baker's permission. The season ended in bitterness, acrimony, and confusion. Caray and Stone left after the season, and Hendry accommodated Baker by eventually trading Sosa to the Baltimore Orioles.

The Cubs were in decline, and things got only worse for Baker in 2005 and 2006. The '05 team dipped below .500 at 79–83, and the '06 team completely collapsed, finishing 66–96. Baker was in the final year of his contract, and during a mid-season series at Houston, beat writers noticed that Hendry had made a list of possible managerial candidates. Baker seemed both defiant and resigned to his fate as the season slogged to its sorry conclusion.

The Cubs announced they were not renewing Baker's contract, but it was a firing for all intents and purposes. MacPhail announced his resignation after 12 seasons as team president on the final day of the season. Longtime marketing guru John McDonough took over as president and gave Hendry an open checkbook to rebuild the team with free agents for 2007.

For the most part, players remained solidly in Baker's corner. Lee, in particular, repeatedly called him a great manager. Despite Baker's reputation as being tough on pitchers, Wood said he would go through a wall for Baker. When Baker came back as an opposing manager, he and Wood would share a warm embrace and several minutes of friendly conversation on the field during batting practice.

Baker's reputation survived his experience with the Cubs. He took a year off from managing and went on to skipper the Cincinnati Reds, Washington Nationals, and Houston Astros, and each team made the postseason under his guidance. He led the Astros to a World Series title in 2022. That may be enough to eventually punch Baker's ticket to Cooperstown as a Hall of Fame manger. His legacy in Chicago could have been and probably should have been much different. An inch or two either way on an October night in 2003, and it might have been.

6

Sweet Lou

THE WORD MOST OFTEN USED TO DESCRIBE LOU PINIELLA when the Chicago Cubs hired him to replace Dusty Baker was "fiery." If Dusty was California cool, Lou was Florida sunburn hot.

Or so the story went.

Piniella was 63 when the Cubs hired him as their manager after the 2006 season and—try as he might—he could not outrun those images of him being a base-tossing, relief pitcher-rasslin' taskmaster. His clubhouse takedown of pitcher Rob Dibble while Piniella was manager of the Cincinnati Reds is the stuff of legend.

The truth about Piniella is a lot more complicated. Certainly, the fire still burned inside of Sweet Lou, but in the later stages of his life, that fire was more of a controlled burn. And when the flames did burn out of control, it was because Piniella set the blaze intentionally to, well, light a fire under his players. Piniella also is a very sensitive and compassionate man, one who took time out of his busy spring training day to give a hug to a beat writer whose father had just died.

Pitcher/author Jim Bouton sized up Piniella quite well more than 50 years ago, when the two were teammates in spring training with the Seattle Pilots (who foolishly traded Piniella to the Kansas City Royals, where Piniella kick-started a career as a solid major league player).

"Piniella has the red ass," Bouton wrote in his landmark book, *Ball Four*. "He doesn't think he's been playing enough... He says he knows they don't want him and that he's going to quit baseball rather than go back to Triple A. He hits the hell out of the ball. He hit a three-run homer today and he's got a .400 average, but they're easing him out. He complains a lot about the coaches and ignores them when he feels like it and, to top it off, he's sensitive as hell to things like [Pilots manager] Joe Schultz not saying good morning to him."

Piniella had managed for 16 straight years with Cincinnati, the Seattle Mariners, and the Tampa Bay Devil Rays (following a previous three-year stint with the New York Yankees) before taking the 2006 season off to recharge by working as a TV analyst on FOX's national telecasts. But that fire still burned, and on October 17, 2006, Cubs general manager Jim Hendry introduced Piniella at a Wrigley Field news conference.

The aim was to win right away, and the timing was fortuitous for Piniella. The Tribune Co., which owned the Cubs, decided to pump millions into player payroll. Nobody knew it at the time, but a few months later, the Trib announced that the Cubs were up for sale. The Trib was trying to increase the asking price by putting a more attractive team on the field. The way to do that was to buy better and more expensive players. With players such as Alfonso Soriano now on board with an eight-year, $136 million deal—a contract as un-Trib-like as it got—the pressure was on to win. Piniella survived and thrived under volatile owners George Steinbrenner in New York and Marge Schott in Cincinnati, so he should have been used to pressure. But the Chicago experience seemed to be something else again. "This is no push-button operation," Piniella marveled one day. He also coined the term "Cubbie occurrence" as a catch-all for those peculiar misfortunes that seemed to befall only the Cubs.

One team executive noted that Piniella wore a look of amazement in the dugout during the latter innings of a week-day game in April, when 40,000 fans screamed in anticipation of an early-season victory. But things got off to a rocky start for Piniella, as the Cubs got off to a 22–31 record by early June. Before one night game in late May, the Cubs' front-office brass marched one by one past the media in the Cubs clubhouse and into Piniella's office. Speculation ran rampant: Piniella was tired. Piniella was going to quit in frustration. Instead, he assured his bosses that if they stuck with it, the Cubs would be okay.

A little dose of Piniella fire lit the fuse on June 2 during a loss to the Atlanta Braves. Cubs base runner Angel Pagan was called out by umpire Mark Wegner at third base on a close play as Pagan tried to advance on a ball that got past the catcher. Third-base coach (and Piniella's eventual managerial succes-sor) Mike Quade argued the call. That was Piniella's cue. He bounded out of the dugout, slammed his cap to the ground, kicked dirt on Wegner, and made like a football placekicker with his cap. Naturally, Piniella was ejected, but the Cubs took off after that on the way to winning the National League Central.

Years later, Quade couldn't help but chuckle at what Piniella told him after the game. "Skip looked at me and said, 'You know…you were wrong,'" Quade said.

In other words, Piniella knew the umpire made the right call, but desperate times required desperate measures. Even so, Piniella always downplayed the need to show fire. At one point he quipped: "What do I need to show fire for? I'm not a dragon."

The Cubs wound up winning the National League Central with a record of 85–77. The clincher came on a Friday night in Cincinnati, where the Cubs won 6–0 behind Carlos Zambrano. Before the Cubs clinched, Piniella summed up the season aptly. "We've been playing good baseball for a long time after a slow start," he said. "You check our record from the first of June on, it's been very representative. It's been good. I felt all along that in September we'd get hot, and we have."

The Cubs wound up playing—and being swept in three games—by the Arizona Diamondbacks in the National League Division Series. Piniella made the inexplicable move of pulling Zambrano after six innings and 85 pitches of a 1–1 ballgame in the series opener in Phoenix. Reliever Carlos Marmol gave up two runs in the seventh, and the Diamondbacks went on to win 3–1. Piniella said he was saving Zambrano for a possible Game Four, a game that never took place. Asked by Bruce Miles if he would be accused of panicking, Piniella responded sharply: "I'm accused of nothing, sir."

Almost all reporters who covered Piniella loved doing so. First of all, he was a colorful quote. Second, he was easy to transcribe. He talked slowly, often beginning sentences with, "Look," before expounding. He also liked to think out loud while gathering his thoughts by injecting, "And, and, and, and" between words. But as writers who covered Piniella in the past warned their colleagues in Chicago, if he used a "Sir" or a "My friend" in a reply, that reporter was in for a scorching. "You think we're stupid?" he shot back at a question about strategy.

"What kind of baseball do you play?" he barked at another question he deemed hostile or born of second-guessing.

Try as he might, Piniella could not get the job completely done in Chicago. His 2008 club went 97–64, including 55–26 at Wrigley Field. But they were swept again—this time by the Joe Torre-led Los Angeles Dodgers—and they looked tight during the series. Piniella wanted badly to win while with the Cubs, and perhaps the players sensed that urgency and couldn't play in a relaxed manner.

In 2009 Piniella had the Cubs in first place as late as August, but the run was over, and the Cubs finished the season 83–78, second in the division, and out of the playoffs. Moreover, stress appeared to be taking a toll on Piniella, who was saddled with outfielder Milton Bradley on the roster. Bradley was a controversial figure whom Hendry signed in hopes that the stability of a three-year contract would help Bradley settle down and use his on-base ability to help the Cubs. But Bradley played inattentive baseball at times, and Piniella berated him in the runway between the dugout and clubhouse during a game against the Chicago White Sox. In September, Bradley was suspended and sent home by Hendry after Bradley made disparaging comments about the Cubs to the *Daily Herald*.

Piniella became naturally preoccupied by his mother's illness in 2010, leaving the club once and eventually retiring. He and his players both seemed to tire of each other. Before one game, Piniella wore his Yankees championship ring to the park. Before another, he tossed out to reporters that the players were enjoying caviar in the clubhouse.

On balance, Piniella got the Cubs to the postseason two years in a row and brought excitement to the North Side. During his job interview, he was asked if he would be open to playing young players, something Baker seemed reluctant to do. Piniella said he would and he made good on his word by giving opportunities to the likes of Ryan Theriot (.387 on-base percentage in 2008) and to catcher Geovany Soto, who came up late in 2007 and won Rookie of the Year honors in 2008.

Piniella also knew who could play and who couldn't and who would take instruction and who wouldn't. Theriot's opportunity came when Piniella had seen enough of veteran Cesar Izturis at shortstop. And when Piniella deemed Hendry favorite Michael Barrett not good enough defensively behind the plate, the catcher was shipped out, eventually opening the door for Soto.

Even though Piniella was a professional hitter and a hitting coach at heart, he also knew a thing a two about pitching, perhaps from years of facing them at the plate. One day during his first spring training with the Cubs, Piniella asked pitching coach Larry Rothschild to move a pitcher from the center of the rubber to the third-base side of the rubber. "Just to give the hitters a different angle," Piniella told the writers who noticed the change while standing behind the batting cage during the practice session.

Piniella may have looked at the Cubs job as the ultimate opportunity and challenge: get this franchise a World Series victory and maybe it would get him to Cooperstown as a manager, something he may deserve anyway because of his work in other cities. Hendry had nothing but praise for Piniella when it was all over. "He realized as much anyone that we were not just running a major league baseball team; we're running an organization," Hendry said. "He did a great job of incorporating an entire organization and the young coaches and players. He also helped develop a lot of players."

7

The Curse Buster

THE CHICAGO CUBS ENTERED THE OFFSEASON OF 2014–15 IN no apparent need of a new manager. Ricky Renteria, who had been hired a year earlier to replace Dale Sveum, seemed to have done the job team president Theo Epstein and general manager Jed Hoyer hired him to do. That is: be the good cop to young players such as Starlin Castro and Anthony Rizzo in contrast to the bad cop played by Sveum, who threatened both young stars with demotion to the minor leagues early in the 2013 season. Those remarks proved to be the beginning of the end for Sveum.

The Cubs' record from 2013–14 improved from 66–96 under Sveum to 73–89 under the mild-mannered and bilingual Renteria, who was able to communicate with Castro and other Latin American players. At a fan event shortly after 2014 the season ended, the Cubs announced that well-regarded hitting coach John Mallee would be joining Renteria's staff for 2015.

Then things changed dramatically.

Shortly after the Mallee announcement, a bombshell exploded in Tampa Bay. Rays general manager Andrew Friedman announced he was going to resign to take the same job with the Los Angeles Dodgers. Maddon, who had been Rays manager since 2006, had an out in his contract, and when news broke that he would not be joining Friedman in L.A., the natural speculation began in all of the Chicago media that Epstein and Hoyer would target Maddon. When there was radio silence from the Cubs front office, media members correctly read this as meaning their initial instincts were correct.

The bottom line was this: the Cubs were either going to hire Maddon or die trying. After all, Maddon was perfect for the situation the Cubs found themselves in: a young team that appeared ready to contend—if not win—right away.

Epstein and Hoyer swung into action. On Friday, November 1, the Cubs announced the firing of Renteria along with a news conference for the following Monday to announce Maddon's hiring. The rapidity of the moves suggested to some that the Cubs had been guilty of illegal tampering with Maddon, but they eventually were cleared of such charges. To woo Maddon, Epstein and Hoyer flew down to Florida to meet him at his RV. They knew that Maddon was a wine lover, but they had forgotten to bring a bottle as an ice-breaking present. So they found themselves scrounging the shelves of a Publix store to find something suitable for Maddon's sophisticated palate. Evidently, they found the right grape—cheap as it might have been. The shot-and-beer press conference at the Cubby Bear was vintage Maddon, and he trotted out the lines that would become repeated over and over during the next five years. "Never permit the pressure to exceed the pleasure...It's all about setting your standards, your goals high because the problem if you don't set them high is you might actually hit your mark," he said. "We need to set our mark high absolutely. I'm going to talk playoffs. I'm going to talk World Series. This year I am. I promise you. And I'm going to believe it."

The media members on hand at the old bar ate it up even if they didn't drink it up, declining Maddon's offer of shots and beers. Given the touchy and, to some, cruel nature of Renteria's dismissal, both Epstein and Maddon did their parts to praise the work manager did.

This was going to be fun. After all, Maddon had a history of working well with young players in Tampa Bay with the Rays, whom he guided to the 2008 World Series. The Cubs added a big dose of credibility in December of 2014 when they signed pitcher Jon Lester to a six-year, $155 million contract.

Maddon's biggest task would be to get the overall young squad to believe—to believe in itself, to believe it could win, and to believe it could beat the St. Louis Cardinals. The Cubs lost three of four to the Cardinals at Busch Stadium from May 4–7 to fall to 14–13, but Maddon used the rest of the season to build the confidence of his troops. "A mind once stretched has a difficult time going back to its original form," was another of Maddon's sayings. In other words, believe you can do something, and those old doubts melt away.

On July 25 the Cubs and their ascending ace, Jake Arrieta, were no-hit at Wrigley Field by the Philadelphia Phillies' Cole Hamels. The Cubs lost again the next day, but a come-from-behind, walk-off win against the Colorado Rockies on July 27 seemed to awaken them. Then came the series that Maddon pointed to as the turning point of the Cubs' season and of their own rise: a four-game sweep of the San Francisco Giants at Wrigley Field. The series finale was a 2–0 victory by Arrieta, whose record improved to 13–6.

The breakthrough Maddon was looking for against the Cardinals came when his Cubs took two of three from their

Gateway Arch Rivals from September 18 to 20 at Wrigley Field. And just as Dusty Baker did in late 2003, Maddon was ready to tell the Cardinals that his boys were no longer their punching bags. In the game on September 18, the Cardinals hit Cubs batter Rizzo twice—once after Cubs soft-tosser Dan Haren plunked Matt Holliday.

Bruce Miles knew Maddon wanted to go off. So after a few general questions about the game from other reporters, Miles asked about the hit batters. Maddon seemed ready for the question and he did not disappoint with his answer. "I'm really disappointed in what the Cardinals did right there," he said. "Absolutely, we did not hit their guy on purpose at all. That was an absolute mistake. There's no malicious intent whatsoever on Dan Haren's part. None. So to become this vigilante group that all of a sudden wants to get their own pound of flesh, that's absolutely insane, ridiculous, and wrong. Furthermore, we don't start stuff, but we will stop stuff. We will end stuff. That's their call. That was their moment right there."

The Cardinals were known for having the self-proclaimed "best fans in baseball" and for playing the game the "right way." Maddon took aim at all that, too. "I never read that particular book that the Cardinals wrote way back in the day," he said. "I'm a big Branch Rickey fan, but I never read the book the Cardinals had written on how to play baseball...Furthermore, that particular book you guys got was written right around the turn of the last century, like 1900, when it took several singles to score a run as opposed to one big guy coming up and hitting a home run."

Mission accomplished, at least to this point. Maddon had succeeded in getting the Cubs to believe they could beat the Cardinals anytime, anyplace. The Cubs didn't win the division, but thanks to two wild-card spots, they were able to make the playoffs as the third-place team in the National League Central behind the first-place Cardinals and the second-place Pittsburgh Pirates. Arrieta took care of the Pirates with a complete-game gem in the single-game, wild-card playoff in Pittsburgh.

Next up were those Cardinals in the National League Division Series. Kyle Schwarber's home run to the top of the right-field videoboard helped the Cubs complete their triumph against the Cardinals (any many demons) as they won that best-of-five series in four games. Although the Cubs were swept in four games in the National League Championship Series by the New York Mets, there was feeling that the next step was just ahead and that the Cubs were ready to take it successfully. The talk in many media circles was that the Cubs had "arrived ahead of schedule." In other words, they weren't supposed to have made the postseason this soon. For that, Maddon got much of the credit.

Maddon and Epstein played it just right the following spring. Both said the Cubs had won nothing other than third place in their division in 2015. The Cubs took a businesslike approach to spring training and swept the Angels in Anaheim in two games to start the 2016 season.

Maddon also let his players play in 2016. Fortified with veterans such as 2015 World Series winner Ben Zobrist from the Kansas City Royals and Jason Heyward from the hated Cardinals, the Cubs won the National League Central with a record of 103–58, surviving a midseason bump in the road.

All the while, Maddon was keeping things loose with themed dress-up road trips and something called American Legion Week during the dog days of summer. Maddon wanted his players to come and play the game, much as they did when they played American Legion ball in high school. That meant not showing up for games until a couple of hours before first pitch and eschewing (to use a favorite word of Maddon's) batting practice, which he called "the most overrated exercise in baseball." (The Cubs skipped regular batting practice on many days throughout Maddon's tenure.)

This time, the Cubs would not sneak up on anybody in the postseason. They clinched the Division Series in a hard-fought win over the Giants in Game Four. Maddon said he feared going back home for a Game Five against tough Giants pitcher Johnny Cueto.

Next up in the National League Championships Series were the Dodgers, winners of 91 games in 2016. The Cubs won their first National League pennant since 1945 on October 22 at Wrigley Field with a 5–0 victory behind the pitching of Kyle Hendricks and the hitting of Willson Contreras and Rizzo, each of whom hit solo homers off Dodgers ace Clayton Kershaw.

Maddon had guided the Cubs to the World Series, and even though the Cubs eventually won their first world championship since 1908, Maddon's managing would come under scrutiny seemingly forevermore. Down three games to one in the World Series, the Cubs rallied to win Game Five at Wrigley Field and Game Six at Cleveland against the American League champion Indians.

Almost all of the second-guessing of Maddon centered on his handling of the pitching staff. In the 3–2 victory in Game Five, Maddon used closer Aroldis Chapman for two-and-two-thirds innings. In the 9–3 victory in Game Six at Cleveland, Maddon turned to Chapman for one-and-one-third innings after two were out in the seventh inning. Maddon and the Cubs were going to ride Chapman hard after trading for him at midseason in a deal with the New York Yankees. They weren't going to re-sign Chapman, so the mentality was to use the hard-throwing left-hander for all he was worth.

In the now-famous Game Seven, Maddon pulled starting pitcher Hendricks after only four-and-two-thirds innings, opting for Lester in relief with the Cubs holding a 5–1 lead. Lester, a throwback who would take the ball in any situation, wound up working three innings, giving up two runs, one of them unearned. Maddon again went to Chapman—this time in the bottom of the eighth with the Cubs holding a 6–3 lead with two outs and the Indians having a man on base. Chapman, operating on fumes, gave up an RBI double to Brandon Guyer and a game-tying homer to Rajai Davis, a blast that had Cubs fans around the world groaning, "Here we go again." Writers in the Progressive Field press box were rewriting their stories on deadline.

Chapman suffered a blown save, but he got out of further trouble in the eighth inning and worked a 1–2–3 ninth, eventually getting credit for the win as the Cubs rallied for an 8–7 victory in 10 innings after the fabled 17-minute rain delay and an inspirational weight room speech by Heyward. Maddon steadfastly defended his decisions, repeatedly saying he was going with his best reliever because there was "no Game Eight."

The Cubs returned to the NLCS in 2017, falling to the Dodgers. They needed a Game 163 to gain wild-card spot in 2018. With an offense that was sputtering, the Cubs fell to the Colorado Rockies in the wild-card game. The end for Maddon with the Cubs came at the conclusion of the 2019 season, when the Cubs missed the playoffs, and the team decided not to extend his contract. In essence, Maddon was fired. He was the only member of the Cubs key baseball management team—Epstein, Hoyer, and Jason McLeod, the chief of scouting and player development—not to have received a contract extension.

Maddon got official word he would not be back on the final Saturday night of the season, when Maddon and Epstein emptied at least one, and probably more, bottles of wine—and not the stuff on the bottom shelf at Publix.

For all of the gnashing of teeth over Maddon's handling of pitching, which many fans feel nearly cost the Cubs their World Series title, one thing often gets overlooked: Maddon never panicked after his team got down three games to one. He was the same guy before and after every game. The beat writers covering the team would meet with Maddon in his office separately before every postseason game. Invariably, Maddon would be relaxed with either music playing or the TV on. The group would chat about the upcoming game and things ranging from world events to Maddon saying he thinks about the fan who sits in the far reaches of the upper deck. (Miles took a photo from that seat at Wrigley Field and showed it to Maddon, who asked for a copy of the photo and then sent a thank you note to the writer.) It was all in keeping with Maddon's philosophy of not getting to high for any one game—whether it was on March 18, May 18, August 18, or October 18.

Maddon was never afraid of the unconventional, such as batting the pitcher eighth instead of ninth or using the burly and power-hitting Schwarber as the leadoff hitter. When Schwarber failed in that role and was sent to the minor leagues briefly in 2017, neither he nor Maddon blamed the experiment for Schwarber's demotion. In fact, when Schwarber went on to play for other teams, his managers did not shy away from using him in the leadoff spot to take advantage of his power and on-base ability. So maybe Maddon was ahead of his time on Schwarber. Whatever, Maddon never shied away from the criticism that came with that decision or others, saying he welcomed the barroom discussions. If that was born of Maddon having spent some time in barrooms, so be it. When the details are long forgotten, fans will read the names of managers who tried and failed to win a World Series with the Cubs. That all ended with Joe Maddon.

PART 3

THE TRADES

8

Brock for Broglio

On June 17, 1962, a sunny, sultry 90-degree Sunday afternoon in Upper Manhattan, a young Chicago Cubs outfielder named Lou Brock flashed all the tools that would make him a Hall of Famer. In the first game of a doubleheader against the first-year New York Mets at the Polo Grounds, Brock stepped up in the first inning and hit a two-run home run to the bleachers just to the right of straightaway center field.

Know this about center field at the horseshoe/bathtub-shaped Polo Grounds: the center-field fence was 475 feet from home plate. (Because of the odd shape of this fabled ballpark, the wall at the left-field line was only 279 feet from the plate, and the wall at the right-field line was a cozy 257.67 feet from home. The center-field bleachers jutted forward from the dead center mark toward home plate. Brock's homer initially was estimated to have traveled 470 feet. Later accounts, as often happens, had the blast traveling some 480 feet.) In other words, Brock's blast was a mammoth one, and it was only the third homer hit to near dead center. Babe Ruth had done so in 1921, and Joe Adcock hit one in 1953. In the Negro Leagues, Luke Easter homered to that area in 1948.

Brock's homer was so monumental that the next day's edition of the *Chicago Tribune* featured an illustration of the trajectory of the ball off the bat. The headlines and subheads reflected the enormity of the home run: "Brock hits historic homer in sweep of Mets series" and "Brock's historic homer some sock by Brock and Cubs!" Richard Dozer, the *Tribune*'s Cubs beat writer began his story this way: "The Chicago Cubs, mind you, have a four-game winning streak; their head coach, Charlie Metro, is back to the .500 level as a manager, and Lou Brock, their deceivingly powerful rookie center fielder, has earned a page in the 50-year history of the Polo Grounds. All these achievements took place today, as the ninth-place Cubs swept a doubleheader from the last-place Mets, 8–7 and 4–3."

Brock, it seemed, had no idea what he had accomplished when the ball left the bat, but he recalled the moment years later in an interview with the *Trib*'s Jerome Holtzman, the "dean" of Chicago baseball writers. "The pitch was over my head, fastball with a lot of backspin. I chopped down on it and began running as fast as I could," Brock told Holtzman. "Bill Jackowski, the second-base umpire, gave me the home run sign. I thought he meant if I kept on running, I'd have an inside-the-park homer. I came around home plate as fast as I could. Nobody shook my hand. All the Cubs were looking out to the outfield. [Ron] Santo then began pounding me and said, 'Did you see where the ball went? Did you see the ball? Way up there.' I looked to where he was pointing. I remember saying to myself, *I need binoculars*."

Brock's day wasn't done in in the doubleheader, as Dozer recounted: "In game two the Cubs were gifted with single unearned runs in the fourth and sixth to stay close to the Mets...A burst of speed by Brock was responsible for one run as he streaked all the way home from second while Andre Rodgers was being thrown out by the catcher." Brock scored despite twisting his knee, an injury that forced him from the game an inning later.

Power, potential, and speed. Brock showed them all on that day for the Cubs as he did for his entire Hall of Fame career. Alas, that Hall of Fame career blossomed not with the Cubs— but elsewhere.

* * *

Brock for Broglio.

That's all anybody has to say to any fan of the Chicago Cubs or the St. Louis Cardinals.

Brock for Broglio.

You don't even need first names.

The Cubs woke up on June 15, 1964, an off day in the schedule, with a record of 27–27 and in sixth place in the 10-team National League, five-and-a-half games out of first place. It was a respectable record for a team that rebounded in 1963 to finish 82–80 after going 59–103 in 1962. The '63 season was the first time since 1946 that the Cubs had finished above .500.

Before the '64 season, the Cubs were shocked to hear that their young second baseman, Ken Hubbs, the Rookie of the Year in 1962, was killed piloting his own plane in Utah.

Based on the 1963 season, there was reason for some hope. Ernie Banks, who had moved from shortstop to first base full time in 1962, was still formidable at 33 years old. Young players Ron Santo and Billy Williams were budding stars. Lou Brock had shown flashes of brilliance since coming to the big leagues.

Cubs general manager John Holland felt his team could be a contender in a wide-open National League. What Holland felt they needed was pitching. The '63 team featured stylish left-hander Dick Ellsworth, who went 22–10 with a 2.11 ERA. Veterans Larry Jackson and Bob Buhl (of World Series fame with the Milwaukee Braves in 1957 and 1958) were back for '64. Also pitching for the Cubs in '64 was Lew Burdette, Buhl's World Series teammate with the Braves. Burdette had just come to the Cubs from the Cardinals in a trade for pitcher Glen Hobbie, one of several hard-throwing pitching prospects the Cubs once had hoped would carry them deep into the 1960s. Although the Cubs were seeking to fortify their pitching in mid-June, the rotation was more than holding its own: Ellsworth at the time was 8–5 with a 3.05 ERA, Buhl was 7–3 with a 3.40 ERA, Jackson was 8–4 with a 3.47 ERA, and Burdette was 2–1 with a 3.72 ERA.

While some Cubs were enjoying a Monday on the golf course on June 15, Holland pulled off a stunner, sending Brock and pitchers Jack Spring and Paul Toth to the Cardinals for Broglio, pitcher Bobby Shantz, and outfielder Doug Clemens. The trade was a shock to the system of the Cardinals, who were 28–30 and six-and-a-half games out of first place and in seventh on the morning of June 15.

Despite what we know about the trade today, the reaction to the deal was swift on June 15 and in the days afterward, and most observers thought the Cubs had gotten the best of the deal. After all, the soon-to-be 29-year-old Broglio was 18–8 in 1963 with an ERA of 2.99. He was a 21-game winner in 1960, finishing third in the voting for the Cy Young Award and ninth in MVP voting. "This gives us as good a pitching staff as there is in the league," Cubs head coach Bob Kennedy told the *Chicago Tribune* at the time.

The *Chicago Daily News* was euphoric over what Holland had just pulled over on his GM counterpart, Bing Devine, in St. Louis. "Thank you, thank you, oh, you lovely St. Louis

Cardinals," a column began. "Nice doing business with you. Please call again any time."

In St. Louis the arrival of Brock was greeted with some skepticism. The *Tribune*'s Jerome Holtzman recalled in a 1996 column that Bill White, the Cardinals' veteran first baseman and later president of the National League, "remembers that none of the St. Louis players liked the deal." Holtzman also reported that some fans in St. Louis "carried a banner that read: 'Broglio for Brock. Who could make such a deal?'"

Who indeed? "With the Brock trade, it was not widely criticized from a Cubs perspective at the time it was made," said research historian Ed Hartig. "Was that a reasonable reaction at the time, considering Brock hadn't blossomed, Broglio was a proven pitcher, and that the Cubs needed pitching to stay in the race coming off an encouraging 1963 season? In hindsight, the trade was awful for the Cubs. There are many players, reporters, and fans from the era who will tell you that they said it was a bad trade when it happened. That's revisionist history. The overwhelming consensus at the time was that the Cubs got the better of the deal, and what are the Cardinals doing? The Cubs had a need and they went out and filled it. They traded away a guy who struck out too often and struggled playing right field at Wrigley for a pitcher with a proven track record."

Those Cubs players, who were golfing at the time, recalled being surprised by the deal. "It was real shocking," Cubs Hall of Famer Williams told the *Tribune* years later. "I think back on that trade, and Ernie, Santo, and I were all driving in runs, and Holland thought we needed pitching. Broglio had won 30 ballgames in '62 and '63. We were scoring runs, and the Cubs didn't think Lou was going to be the player he was."

Although Kennedy in later years insisted he and his coaches were against the trade, that assessment goes against the reporting of the day. "Brock had fallen into some disfavor with Kennedy, a stickler for sound application of baseball's fundamentals," wrote *Tribune* beat writer Dick Dozer after news of the trade broke. "Kennedy was irritated at times, however, by Brock's erratic outfield play and occasionally by his unsound base running." Dozer, a perceptive writer during decades on the baseball beat, did issue one ominous warning, writing: "Possessed of tremendous speed, Brock could prove to be a sound investment for the Cardinals. He turns 25 [on June 18, 1964]. He is hitting .250 this season and he leads the Cubs in stolen bases with 10 already."

The trade was win for the Cardinals—both in the long term and short term—and it was as if a switch was flipped with Brock from the moment he got to St. Louis. For the rest of the 1964 season, Brock went .348/.387/.527 with 12 home runs, 44 RBIs, and 33 stolen bases. It's fair to say Brock was the catalyst for the Cardinals winning the National League pennant and the World Series. Although the Cardinals were 11–18 in June, they went 17–11 in July, 18–10 in August, and 21–8 in September. They trailed the Philadelphia Phillies by six-and-a-half games on September 20, as the Phillies had 12 games to play, and the Cardinals had 13 to play. After September 20 the Phillies lost 10 straight games while the Cardinals won nine of 10 on their way to the pennant and an eventual seven-game World Series victory against the New York Yankees. (While the Cardinals were struggling to catch the Phillies in August, team owner August Busch fired Devine as general manager, replacing him with Bob Howsam. It was a cruel twist for Devine.)

Unlike his time in Chicago, Brock knew where he stood with the Cardinals and their manager, Johnny Keane, who took the brakes off his young outfielder, allowing him freedom on the base-paths. "Here's a young guy with two left feet who doesn't know where he's going, and I was traded for a 21-game winner," Brock told the *Tribune* years later. "I knew the kind of quality pitcher [Broglio] was. Until the trade, I had no idea of my value in baseball, what my stock was worth. It gave me some indication how good I might be. It solidified my confidence. The day before the trade, I hit a two-run homer to win a ballgame 5–2 [against the Pittsburgh Pirates]. So I was feeling pretty good. But most of the time, I was worrying, thinking I might get sent back to the minors."

Brock played through the 1979 season, compiling a batting line of .293/.343/.410 with 149 home runs, 900 RBIs, 3,023 hits, and 938 stolen bases, the most all time when Brock retired. His 118 steals in 1974 broke Maury Wills' single season record of 104 set in 1962. Brock's career wins above replacement was 45.3, including 41.7 with the Cardinals. He helped the Cardinals win World Series titles in 1964 and 1967 and a National League pennant in 1968. Brock led the National League in stolen bases eight times, including at age 35. Despite having great speed in his younger years, Brock always said it took him several seasons to learn how to be an effective base stealer. The need to read pitchers and catchers, he said, was just as important as being fast on the base paths. He was a first-ballot Hall of Famer, gaining 79.7 percent of the vote (with 75 percent needed for election) by the Baseball Writers Association of America in 1985.

As for Broglio, both the short-term and long-term returns were disastrous for him and the Cubs. He went 4–7 with a 4.04 ERA after the trade. Instead of contending for the pennant, the Cubs finished the season with a record of 76–86 and in eighth place, 17 games behind the Cardinals. In 1965 Broglio was 1–6 with a 6.93 ERA. His career was over after the 1966 season, when he was 2–6 with a 6.35 ERA in a season when the Cubs finished 59–103. While Brock was on his way to a Hall of Fame career in St. Louis, Broglio's Cubs career ended with a record of 7–19 with an ERA of 5.40. His WAR with the

Cubs was minus 1.5. It should be noted that while with the Cardinals, Broglio had a record of 70–55 with an ERA of 3.43.

On the surface the Cubs had every right to believe they were getting a quality pitcher. The problem was Broglio's right arm, which apparently had been acting up in 1963. In 2017 Broglio, who died in 2019, told the *Tribune*'s Mark Gonzales: "I had 18 cortisone shots in my shoulder in 1963. Plus, what they were shooting in my elbow."

Broglio underwent surgery on the elbow after the 1964 season, but he may have tried to rush back the following spring. That the trade happened at all can be chalked up to the times. Back in 1964, teams did not routinely share medical information on players involved in trades as is the custom today. "It would've never happened today," Williams told the *Tribune* years later. "We got damaged goods when Ernie Broglio came here. If it happened today, we've got so many doctors that would've checked him out to see if he was sound, and it would've negated the trade."

In later years, Kennedy claimed he and his coaches didn't want to trade Brock. "We just liked Lou Brock a lot more than that," Kennedy told the *Tribune*. "And we didn't want Broglio. Lew Burdette was on our club then and told us Broglio had been having arm problems; he'd been getting shots."

* * *

As painful as the Lou Brock trade is for Chicago Cubs fans, the what-ifs are simply delicious to contemplate. The biggest is this: would Brock have blossomed into a Hall of Famer with the Cubs had they not traded him to the St. Louis Cardinals?

In 1974 Brock told *Chicago Tribune* columnist Robert Markus that he felt he "arrived" shortly before the trade was made, citing a catch he made while climbing the Wrigley Field vines in right field. "I'd have made it as a big league player in any event," he told Markus. "And I would have eventually been a base stealer for the Cubs...When I came up to the big leagues, remember, I was raw. I had two left feet. The first time I ever hit leadoff was when I came to the major leagues. But I had about 10 steals for the Cubs already that year I was traded. When I got to St. Louis, Johnny Keane, the manager, asked me if I could steal bases. I lied to him and told him yes. And he gave me the green light to steal."

While Keane was the manager of the Cardinals, the Cubs were still using a "head coach" (Bob Kennedy) as part of their infamous "College of Coaches," a cockamamie concept introduced for the 1961 season following the Cubs' 14th consecutive sub-.500 season. Cubs owner P.K. Wrigley shocked the baseball world when he introduced the College of Coaches during the winter of 1960–61. Instead of having one man be the manager (a term Wrigley reportedly found synonymous with dictator), eight coaches would rotate up and down the entire system, and one would be designated as "head coach of the major league club."

Reports say Cubs catcher Elvin Tappe, who began his major league career with the Cubs in 1954, approached Wrigley with the idea of rotating coaches and instructors throughout the minor league system. (Those practices have been commonplace in baseball for decades.) However, Tappe later claimed that he never meant for the rotating coach system to be used at the major league level and that, "Mr. Wrigley got all carried away."

"Mr. Wrigley called me in because I was a holdover coach and asked what I thought they should do," Tappe was quoted as saying in a Fangraphs article. "I had been with the Cubs about five years. We had all those good, young arms, but every time we went to spring training, we had a new pitching coach. And I said, 'We've got to systemize to have stability.' He bought that. I wrote an organizational playbook. He gave me extra money for that. We had the same signs, except for the keys, the same cutoff and rundown plays for all the clubs in our organization. When a player moved up, he didn't have to learn anything new. We taught from kindergarten all the way through graduation, but I never mentioned anything about rotating managers. It was his idea."

Carried away or not, the Cubs began the system with an eight-man College of Coaches: Tappe, Charlie Grimm, Goldie Holt, Bobby Adams, Harry Craft, Verlon "Rube" Walker, Ripper Collins, and Vedie Himsl. Others eventually to join the "faculty" of the College of Coaches were Buck O'Neil, Alvin Dark, Lou Klein, Dick Cole, and Fred Martin, who would gain fame years later for teaching the split-finger fastball to Bruce Sutter, who began his career with the Cubs but went on to a Hall of Fame career after the Cubs (naturally) traded him to St. Louis.

In 1961 the Cubs rolled out their College of Coaches for real, and the team went 64–90, as Himsl, Craft, Tappe, and Klein took turns as head coach. It was during that season that a 22-year-old outfielder named Lou Brock made his major league career on September 10.

Things got worse for the Cubs in 1962, when they went a franchise worst 59–103. Tappe opened the season as head coach, but the Cubs went 4–16 under his stewardship. Klein rotated upward and went 12–18. The Cubs finally settled on Charlie Metro to serve as head coach for the rest of the season, and he posted a record of 43–69.

As for Brock, he put up a batting line of .263/.319/.412 with nine home runs, 35 RBIs, and 16 stolen bases. Another bright spot was 20-year-old second baseman Ken Hubbs, who won both the Rookie of the Year Award and the Gold Glove.

Things got interesting before the 1963 season. The Cubs did not abandon the College of Coaches, but they streamlined it. Wrigley named Kennedy head coach for at least two seasons.

It's a job Kennedy kept until partway through the 1965 season, when he made way for Klein. Years later, when interviewed by the *Daily Herald*, Kennedy vehemently stated that he was the manager of the Cubs, not the head coach, during his tenure at the top step of the dugout.

Also before the '63 season, Wrigley hired a retiring Air Force colonel named Robert Whitlow to be the Cubs' athletic director. Whitlow was an imposing man physically, and Wrigley was reported to have been impressed by his 6'5", 230-pound frame. Whitlow, who later said he came in to end—not continue—the College of Coaches system, said he would be in uniform during games to supervise the team and its coaches. The Whitlow experiment also failed, as he lost a power struggle with Kennedy and was quietly dismissed before the 1965 season. Wrigley sadly noted that Whitlow may have been too far ahead of his time. Whitlow tried to implement such practices as new types of physical conditioning, applied psychology, and special diets that included powdered nutritional supplements—all commonplace today. Kennedy wanted Whitlow nowhere near the players, and that included Brock, whom Whitlow championed as a future star of the Cubs. The 1963 season was a huge improvement for the Cubs, who went 82–80. Brock hit .258/.300/.382 with nine homers, 37 RBIs, and 24 stolen bases.

After Brock was traded the following year, the Cubs soldiered on with their College of Coaches into the 1965 season. Even though the system may have been de-emphasized, the Cubs touted it in their 1965 media guide, writing: "Designed to help speed the development of young players with coaches of major league caliber, the Cubs coaching system was introduced in 1960. Now in its fifth year, it continues to progress toward its goals. Today, more and better instruction and training is or should be the No. 1 goal in all fields. This, together with a standard system of play, are the two main features of the Cubs system. The new system started with eight coaches. As the need for more intensive instruction became evident, the total number has risen to 14. Among the young players produced are Ron Santo, Dick Ellsworth, Don Kessinger, Billy Williams, Glenn Beckert, Cal Koonce, Jim Stewart, and Jack Warner."

The College of Coaches came to emphatic end when the Cubs hired Leo Durocher to be their manager after the 1965 season. Durocher made it quite clear he was there to be the manager—and not the head coach. But by this time, Brock was long gone.

The question on whether Brock would have broken out and had a Hall of Fame career with the Cubs centers on whether he was hampered by the College of Coaches and hearing different things from different instructors. "No," said Tom Shaer, a Chicago media consultant and former TV and radio sports anchor reporter and talk-show host. "The Cardinals had always valued speed. The National League had more speed than the American League. Maury Wills had already shown baseball how speed could change a game. The American League was always slow to get the message. Each league had its own ideas…The American League, if you look at the owners, they were a lot of stodgy owners. Even though the Cubs were in the National League, the Cardinals were a better-run organization. [Brock] said [the Cubs] didn't tell him a different type of ballplayer to be, but with the College of Coaches, 'One day we're going to hit and run. The next day we're not. One month, so and so's going to play center field. So he and I would communicate. I knew what the difference was between a center fielder and a corner outfielder, what we had to do.'

"Now, a new manager comes in, and Brock called it 'the College of Rotating.' They come in, and we've got different guys in different positions. He said, 'We didn't know which end was up half the time.' Look at any star player who needed to be developed, and he was not going to do as well there as he did in St. Louis playing for some pretty good managers. Billy Williams did not need a lot of development. Ron Santo did not need a lot of development. These guys came up and were pretty much turnkey operations who needed just a couple years of getting some at-bats and some ground balls hit your way. I don't see how the Cubs ever nurtured or developed anybody to speak of."

Research historian Ed Hartig also delved into the many what-ifs with Brock and the Cubs. "What if they had waited another year before bringing him up from the minors?" Hartig asked. "What if the Cubs had a manager and not the College of Coaches? What if the Cubs had moved him to left field and Billy Williams to right field? Honestly, I don't think Brock has a Hall of Fame career if he stays with the Cubs."

There may have been one overriding reason for that. "The Cubs simply were not built to take advantage of Lou's greatest weapon—his speed," Hartig said. "They were slow-footed and relied too much on the home run. Let's say they hired Leo Durocher a few years earlier. I still don't think Lou gets turned loose on the bases. Leo was Willie Mays' first manager in the majors. Almost from Day One, Leo called Willie one of the greatest players of all time...yet Leo didn't give Mays carte blanche to run whenever he wanted to. Leo needed to show who was in control. If Leo is putting the brakes on Willie Mays, there's no way he'd give Brock the green light to run whenever he wanted. Instead...Brock gets traded to the Cardinals. Manager Johnny Keane moves him to left field and turns him loose on the bases. The Cardinals win the World Series, and Lou is on his way to 3,000 hits and the Hall of Fame."

It's also interesting to speculate on one of the biggest what-ifs of all: would the Cubs have won a pennant or more if Brock had not been traded and had Hubbs not been killed while piloting his airplane in February of 1964. The Cubs never satisfactorily replaced Brock, but Beckert, a second baseman, came up to the Cubs in 1965 after being drafted from the Boston Red Sox organization in November of 1962. Beckert made four All-Star Games and batted .283 for the Cubs over nine seasons, including a .342 mark in 1971. The biggest what-if Cubs season that comes to mind is 1969, when the Cubs had a nine-game lead in mid-August—only to finish eight games behind the charging "Miracle" New York Mets, who went on to win the World Series.

Do Hubbs and Brock make a difference? "Let's assume Hubbs is at second," Hartig said. "That means Beckert is on the bench. One complaint was that Leo didn't trust his bench, and as a result, several players didn't get enough rest. But Leo loved Glenn Beckert. Glenn had played shortstop and third base in the minors before moving to second base for the Cubs. I assume Leo would have trusted Beck and given Santo and Kessinger some much needed days off while occasionally filling in for Hubbs at second base. As for Brock...which Brock would the '69 Cubs have? The Cubs' Brock or the Cardinals' Brock? If [it's] the Cubs' Brock, then Durocher likely sticks with [veteran Jim] Hickman in right field, and there is little impact. However, if they had the Cardinals' Brock and switched him to left field with Billy [Williams] moving to right field...that's really interesting. Would it have been enough to make up nine games in 1969? Probably not. The '69 Mets were a team of destiny. They were fresh and they had the pitching. Even with Hubbs and a Cardinals' Brock, I think the Mets still win the World Series. Now, would Hubbs and a Cardinals' Brock have been enough to overcome five games in 1970? I would have liked to have seen that!"

9

The Ryno Trade

IF RYNE SANDBERG WAS A "THROW-IN," HE WAS THE BEST "throw-in" in the history of Major League Baseball trades. Longtime fans of the Chicago Cubs can recite the trade by heart: on January 27, 1982, new Cubs general manager Dallas Green traded veteran shortstop Ivan DeJesus to the Philadelphia Phillies for firebrand shortstop Larry Bowa and an infield prospect named Ryne Sandberg, who had made his big league debut the previous September 2 in Atlanta and gotten his first hit against the Cubs at Wrigley Field on September 27.

DeJesus was a good-fielding shortstop who had been with mostly bad Cubs teams since 1977. Bowa, a member of the Phillies since 1970, was well known to Green, who managed the Phillies to a World Series title in 1980. Although Green was very familiar with Sandberg from his days in the Phillies front office, few in Chicago knew much about the quiet kid from Spokane, Washington. Writing about the trade in the *Chicago Tribune*,

Jerome Holtzman observed: "The trade for quality shortstops had been in the works for more than a month but wasn't consummated until the Phillies agreed to add Ryne Sandberg, a 22-year-old middle infielder with good speed and a light bat. From the beginning, the Cubs insisted there would be no deal unless Sandberg was included."

Holtzman was known as the "dean" of Chicago baseball writers and he knew full well Sandberg was no throw-in. But others may be forgiven if they viewed Sandberg as something as afterthought. Years later, Sandberg is able to laugh at the notion that he was a throw-in. "Larry Bowa used to joke about me being a throw-in as he was the main player," Sandberg said in 2022. "Ivan DeJesus was the other major leaguer at the time. I was just a minor league player. As I got to know Larry and be friends with him and start my career here, we'd do some things. He came up with the 'throw-in' line, which I kind of took and ran with from a veteran guy like him. But I think what happened there—I know what happened there—Dallas Green was the farm director in '77 and '78 for the Phillies. So he was scouting me and having me scouted by Bill Harper and Moose Johnson. When I was drafted by the Phillies in the 20th round, I had already committed to be a quarterback at Washington State University."

Sandberg was part of something far larger that Green had in mind for awakening the slumbering giant that was the Chicago Cubs in 1981.

* * *

During the summer of 1981, the Wrigley family sold the Chicago Cubs to the Tribune Co. for a reported $20.5 million ($21.1 million, including Wrigley Field). The Cubs were in the midst of strike-interrupted season, in which they would go 38–65. They had not been to the postseason since losing the 1945 World Series to the Detroit Tigers and were going nowhere fast.

On October 15, 1981, the Cubs introduced Dallas Green as their new general manager. Green, a former pitcher with the Philadelphia Phillies, stood 6'5" and was about as subtle as a punch in the mouth, something he looked like he would be glad to deliver at any moment to anyone who looked at him askance. Green's charge was to overhaul everything about the Cubs. Today that would be called "changing the culture," a term much too refined for the earthy (yet savvy) Green.

The Cubs' new marketing slogan under Green was "Building a New Tradition" and it appeared everywhere, including on the team's pocket schedules for the 1982 season. It seemed reasonable enough. Except for a sustained run of winning seasons from 1967 to 1972, which included the epic late-season fall from first place in 1969, the Cubs were losers. But they were "lovable losers," and Green's brash ways and new slogan rubbed some in the public and media the wrong way. How dare this interloper from Philadelphia come here and say this franchise needed to build a new tradition? "Every fan in every city is provincial. There's no question about it," said Tom Shaer, a Chicago-based media consultant and a former TV and radio reporter, anchor, and sports talk-show host. Shaer won his fair share of scoops covering Green's Cubs in the 1980s. "But it doesn't matter where you are. You don't want to be told that you're an idiot. The Cubs were a joke. They were a joke! The Cubs were the laughingstock. And if you're telling people, 'You deserve a winner, and I'm going to do my best to get you a winner,' they're going to love you. But if you say, 'You deserve a winner. I'm going to do my best to give you a winner because you people don't even know what good baseball is,' they don't want to hear that.

"He saw so many things being done wrong. He wanted to tackle it all at once and he was like a bull in a China shop. And he offended people because you don't want to hear that your town is a backwater town with a bunch of losing teams. But that's exactly what Chicago was at the time. Look at the Bears. The Bears were *Brian's Song* and Papa Bear and [sportscasters] Johnny and Jeannie Morris and all that soft, warm, cuddly stuff. And all they did was lose. George Halas was revered. At the time I got here at the end of 1982, his team made one or two playoff games in 20 years. The Blackhawks were mediocre. The Bulls were crummy."

According to Shaer, the message was right. But Green's delivery may have been a little too harsh for the sensibilities of Cubs fans of that time. "I think what happened was: you can't tell people, 'I know better than you; you have been foolish to put up with this,'" he said. "[Green] never used these words, but he told the fans, 'You guys are stupid.' That wasn't the real Dallas. In fact, Dallas told me many times—many times—that it took him a couple of years to understand the ways of the natives here, the way the people were. He had a lot of appreciation for Wrigley Field. He never wanted every game at night. He wanted 20 or 30 night games. He had appreciation for day baseball. He had appreciation for all of it. It just took him awhile to get there. 'Building a New Tradition.' Honestly, what was the Cubs' tradition before that? It was losing. 'Building a New Tradition. We're going to do things differently.' People don't want to hear that."

Undaunted, Green forged ahead, hiring former Phillies people such as Lee Elia to manage the Cubs and Gordon Goldsberry to rebuild the minor leagues. The Tribune Co. also hired popular broadcaster Harry Caray away from the crosstown White

Sox. And Green knew from the start that for the Cubs to be competitive long term, Wrigley Field would need lights.

Things were going to be different.

Green was only getting started raiding his former club, the Phillies, for talent. On December 8, 1981, he traded starting pitcher Mike Krukow (who would enjoy a solid major league career before becoming broadcaster) to the Phillies for pitchers Dan Larson and Dickie Noles and a hard-nosed infielder-outfielder-catcher named Keith Moreland. He saved his best for late January of 1982, when he pulled off what looked like a simple swap of shortstops: Ivan DeJesus for Larry Bowa and the "throw-in" kid Ryne Sandberg. By that time the Cubs were being called the "Phillies West." Just like they were with the "New Tradition," some Cubs fans were wary of all this brotherly love between Chicago and Philadelphia. "I know some people have criticized us because we've made so many deals with the Phillies," Green told the *Chicago Tribune* at the time of the Sandberg trade. "They've called us the 'Phillies West.' That doesn't bother me. It so happens I know the Phillies organization best. And I'll tell you this: the players that we've got all have good heart, and they'll be bringing that to Chicago."

Sandberg was hardly a throw-in, and it took some doing and some tightrope walking by Green to get him. In the end, though, Green had the upper hand—and he knew it—because Bowa was unhappy with his contract situation in Philadelphia. The Phillies were in the process of being sold, and Bowa believed he had an agreement for a three-year deal with the previous regime, something the new bosses weren't keen on honoring.

Green knew the Phillies had to move Bowa, but he had to be careful not to push too hard for Sandberg. "Bowa was definitely the main target of that trade," Shaer said. "But Dallas Green told me several times he had his eyes on Sandberg and that his only fear was that [scout] Hugh Alexander, who was working for the Phillies [and who later joined Green with the Cubs], would convince the Phillies not to trade Sandberg. The issue with the Phillies was that they had a logjam at second base. They had Manny Trillo. They had Julio Franco coming up. So they had to make a choice. Green told me that his concern was that if he talked too much about Sandberg, even though Sandberg wasn't his focus even though he wanted him...the Phillies would get wise and they would demand another Cubs player in return. He told me he never had any fear of not getting Ryno, but he didn't want to have to pay too much. He thought there was an outside chance they could start to fall in love with Ryno to the point where they wouldn't trade him. But there again, that's your logjam with Franco and Trillo there. Dallas never viewed him as a throw-in, not at all. There was no doubt about his work ethic. He just wanted to know how tough he would be. He was very happy to see he was plenty tough. He just wasn't outwardly tough. He was a quiet, regular guy, but as Dallas put it, 'If I'm in an alley fight, Ryno might not like it, but he would punch the other guy for me.' Dallas knew that he wanted to change shortstops and he knew he could get Bowa only after Bowa had publicly called [new Phillies president] Bill Giles a 'damn liar' regarding a supposedly promised contract extension. Because the Phillies had a clear imperative to trade Bowa, Dallas knew that he held the upper hand and had an even better chance to get Ryno in the deal."

Throw-in or not, the jury was out on Sandberg as far as the Chicago media were concerned. From the *Tribune*'s Jerome Holtzman: "Sandberg, who batted .293 and stole 32 bases with Oklahoma City last year, will get his first shot in center field, but unless the Cubs trade outfielder Steve Henderson, it would seem doubtful that Sandberg will crack the Opening

Day lineup." Holtzman went on to opine that for this trade to work for the Cubs, Sandberg had to crack the lineup in the following two years.

One of the appeals of Sandberg was his versatility. He was talented enough play shortstop, third base, second base, or center field—perhaps not at an All-Star level—but well enough. *Tribune* columnist Bob Verdi, the pre-eminent Chicago wordsmith of the day, described Sandberg as "a minor league prospect Green contends could fill any of the 16 or 17 holes in the Chicago lineup, maybe starting with second base or center field as soon as April 5 in Cincinnati."

From a Philadelphia point of view, it was easy to see the problems facing the Phillies. "Bowa had to go," veteran Phillies beat writer Todd Zolecki wrote in his book titled *The Good, the Bad, and the Ugly*. "But where? Former Phillies manager Dallas Green had started to run the show in Chicago and he had interest. But he said the only way he would send DeJesus to the Phillies was if they included Sandberg. 'We knew we had them over a barrel,' Green said. 'Giles had already made the mistake of telling the world Bowa was gone.' I kept saying, 'Since we were the Little Sisters of the Poor, we had to get a plus in the trade.' Their dilemma with Sandberg was that they weren't sure what position he would play. Most didn't think he could play shortstop. They thought he could be a third baseman—except Mike Schmidt was there. They thought he could be a second baseman—except Manny Trillo was there. They thought maybe he could play one of the corner outfield positions. They even tried him as a center fielder, but that experiment was short-lived."

Looking back on the trade more than 40 years later, Sandberg expressed happiness that his former boss in Philly wanted him that badly. Sandberg, a multisport star at North

Central High School in Spokane, Washington, was taken in the 20th round of the 1978 amateur draft by the Phillies. But he possessed baseball talent worthy of a much higher round in the draft. "Dallas Green was very persistent and said, 'We've drafted you. We took you in the 20th round, but you know we were going to take you in the third round,'" Sandberg said. "'We'd still like to talk to you about signing with the Phillies and going that route. We'd offer you the third-round money.' I gave it some thought. As it turned out, I wanted to be a professional athlete. And that was my chance in some regards right there to sign on the dotted line, maybe spend three or four or five years in the minor leagues, almost like going to college, and take my shot at baseball. That's what I ended up doing. So Dallas Green then became the manager of the Phillies in '80 and won the World Series there. He was the manager there the next year, and after my Triple A season, I was a September call-up. He called me up to the big leagues for my first 30 days in the big leagues. I got my first hit here at Wrigley Field as a Philadelphia Phillie, second game of a doubleheader. I started at shortstop. Dallas finished that season with the Phillies and then he took the GM job with the Cubs. So he knew me as a minor league player. He drafted me. He saw something in me way back in high school that I didn't see or nobody else saw. He handpicked me in making that deal from the Phillies' minor league system. The Phillies let me go. So that all transpired. It was all about Dallas Green."

Even so, the perception of Sandberg being a throw-in remained. "Although there is a narrative that has developed over time that Sandberg was a throw-in, that's not true at all," said research historian Ed Hartig. "He wasn't. A throw-in helps sweeten a deal. In this case, I don't think the deal gets done if Sandberg isn't included in the trade. Sure, the Chicago press didn't know Sandberg—which may explain why he was referred to as a 'throw-in'—he had played only three games against the Cubs late in 1981 with only three at-bats. But Dallas Green and Gordie Goldsberry knew who Ryno was. He was athletic, had good size and range, was a smart base runner, and was only 22. Plus, they knew the Phillies had their own Hall of Famer at third base with Mike Schmidt."

* * *

No one had any way of knowing Ryne Sandberg was on the road to a Hall of Fame career. Hell, at the start of his rookie year, it looked like he might not make it at all. He opened the 1982 season as the Chicago Cubs' starting third baseman, supplanting veteran Ken Reitz, who lasted just one season after the previous regime obtained him and Leon Durham from the St. Louis Cardinals for future Hall of Fame closer Bruce Sutter.

The building of the Cubs' new tradition was going to be a painful one, and it was even more so for Sandberg, who had just one hit in his first 36 at-bats for the Cubs. Sandberg recovered nicely and wound up with a line of .271/.312/.372 with seven home runs, 54 RBIs, and 103 runs scored. He finished sixth in Rookie of the Year voting. As a team the Cubs finished 73–89 and in fifth place in the six-team National League East.

For most of 1982, second base for the Cubs was manned by Bump Wills, son of record-setting base stealer Maury Wills. Bump had a respectable season, going .272/.347/.377 with six homers and 38 RBIs. But the Cubs had other plans for second base, and they involved Sandberg. "I made that first Cubs team out of '82 in spring training and I hit the ball really well, and they were looking for a position for me," Sandberg said in 2022. "I happened to be beat out Ken Reitz, a veteran third baseman who had just had a year or two left potentially. I beat him out, so I played third base for the first five months. I played well over there. September 1 came. They were going to expand the roster, and with a month left in the season, Dallas, along with Lee Elia, called me into the office in San Diego and said, 'Ryno, you've done a great job at third base, but we really like the way your bat fits in and your stealing bases and your range. We've noticed your range at third base.' Well, I was a shortstop before that, so I had range. They said, 'We'd like to move you to second base starting tonight.' So I took one pregame [practice session] with Larry Bowa, doing the double play, talking to him, and all that. So I played the last 30 days of my rookie season at second base and took to it right away."

That's an understatement from the understated Sandberg. He finished the season well enough at second base and in 1983 he began a streak of winning nine straight Gold Gloves. From 1984 to 1993, he made 10 straight National League All-Star teams. And of course, Sandberg's coming out party was the "Sandberg Game" on June 23, 1984, when he hit a pair of game-tying home runs off Sutter and wound up with seven RBIs for the day in a 12–11 victory in 11 innings in a game televised by NBC when its *Game of the Week* was still a big deal. That introduced Sandberg to the wider baseball public. He was becoming the preeminent second baseman of the day.

The position change, along with an increase in power, was working. His home run total rose from eight in 1983 to 19 in 1984, peaking at 40 in 1990, when he enjoyed the first of back-to-back seasons of exactly 100 RBIs. (As for Wills, he never played in the major leagues after 1982, opting to play in Japan in 1983 and '84.)

Moving from third base to second proved to be a wise positional change for Sandberg. "It really set me up for my career as being a Hall of Famer," Sandberg said. "The way that my bat played, I did gain power starting in '84 and continued to have power. I hit for average, RBIs, and stolen bases. But to win my first Gold Glove that very next year in 1983—second year in the major leagues, a Gold Glove winner—and then rattle off eight straight and then add the bat, that started the mold that had me headed toward the Baseball Hall of Fame…So yeah, that changed my whole path and my destiny for where I would be in the game once I was finished playing."

Sandberg compiled a career batting line of .285/.344/.452 with 282 home runs, 1,061 RBIs, and a wins above replacement (WAR) of 68. Of his 282 home runs, 275 were hit as a second baseman, placing him third behind Jeff Kent (354) and Robinson Cano (325) and ahead of Hall of Famers Rogers Hornsby (272) and Joe Morgan (268). In addition to his fielding, Sandberg was fundamentally sound in all facets of the game. His throwing arm was strong and accurate, and he did not throw to the wrong base.

It is surprising that it took Sandberg three tries to make it to Cooperstown, New York. He did so in 2005, earning 76.2 percent of the vote by the Baseball Writers Association of America (75 percent is needed for election). Sandberg garnered 49.2 percent in 2003 and 61.1 percent in 2004.

The position switch from third base to second base paid off for the Cubs. The question remains: if the Cubs don't move Sandberg from third base to second, does he carve out a Hall of Fame career? "When I think of Ryno as a Hall of Famer, I think of defense…his 10 All-Star appearances, his nine Gold Gloves, and seven Silver Sluggers," historian Ed Hartig said. "How do those numbers change if Ryno stays at third base and now he's going against Mike Schmidt, Tim Wallach, Terry Pendleton, Matt Williams, Ken Caminiti? He still wins the 1984 MVP if he's at third base. But for many other seasons, he's not getting the same recognition with Schmidt annually finishing at the top for home runs and RBIs and Pendleton playing in five World Series. Two hundred eighty-two home runs for a second base is HOF-worthy. For a third baseman, probably not."

Of course, there are no right or wrong answers to the Hall of Fame question, but there's no doubt the change of positions had an impact. "It made his career," Tom Shaer, a Chicago-based media consultant and a former TV and radio reporter, anchor, and sports talk-show host said. "It's kind of odd to say it...but second base fit Ryno's personality more than short. [The Cubs] saw that. They knew what they wanted to do with the team. They were correct that they could get a couple more years out of Bowa, and then we'll see. Then we'll figure it out. I think it's another unsung hero thing that Dallas did and his advisers. I think that was a very key move.

"When Ryno went into the Hall of Fame, he invited Dallas as his guest. Ryno took me aside. He said, 'He's here as my guest. He's not here with the Phillies. He's here with me because I appreciated what he did.'"

Green's "New Tradition" outlasted him with the Cubs, who won the National League East in 1984. Injuries decimated the pitching staff in 1985, and the Cubs dropped to fourth place. After losing seasons in 1986 and 1987, the Tribune Co. decided it could live without Green, especially after he chafed at his bosses wanting more corporate oversight of the baseball operation, something that was not in their field of expertise. Green's "resignation" after the 1987 season was really a firing. "There is absolutely, positively no question in my mind that they would have had much more consistent winning records if Dallas had stayed," Shaer said. "All you have to do is look at what he and Gordon Goldsberry did to develop players. And they would have kept developing players. We haven't even talked about Rafael

Palmeiro and Jamie Moyer. They got all these guys. The only mistake Dallas Green made was that he gave pretty good contracts to some older players: Matthews, Moreland, maybe one other guy. So they got stuck with some contracts they shouldn't have got stuck with. Dallas was chasing the rabbit. The last year, he was chasing the rabbit, trying to do a patchwork deal, and I think they finished in last place in '87."

Wrigley Field finally got lights in 1988, when they finished 77–85 and in fourth place. In 1989 they won the National League East again, and Green's fingerprints were all over the roster, which by that time included the likes homegrown products Greg Maddux, Mark Grace, Joe Girardi, Jerome Walton, and Dwight Smith. Also there was Andre Dawson, whom Green signed to a blank contract during spring training of 1987, when it was hard for players to land deals because the owners were involved in collusion to keep salaries down. Dawson went on to win MVP honors for a last-place club in 1987.

Of course, Sandberg was a key member of the 1989 division winners. He put up a line of .290/.356/.497 with 30 home runs, 76 RBIs, and a 6.1 WAR. In 1990 Sandberg had a WAR of 7.1 and in 1991 it was 7.0. Sandberg retired during the 1994 season—only to come back for two more seasons in 1996 and 1997. He remains the most productive second baseman in Cubs history, and many consider him the best second baseman of all time—with respect to Kent, Cano, Hornsby, and Morgan, though many in Cincinnati will cite Morgan's contributions to the Big Red Machine as making him the best.

As far as the trade with the Phillies goes, Bowa provided the Cubs with what they were looking for: leadership during a rebuild. While Sandberg compiled a WAR of 68.1 in his 15 seasons with the Cubs, DeJesus spent three seasons with the Phillies with a WAR of 2.9.

The case can be made that the Sandberg trade was the best in Cubs history, but that's another question up for debate. Although the Cubs get slammed for the 1964 trade of future Hall of Famer Lou Brock to the St. Louis Cardinals for sore-armed pitcher Ernie Broglio, they have made their fair share of good trades and gotten their fair share of steals in addition to Sandberg. Players acquired in those deals included Hall of Famers Ferguson Jenkins and Mordecai "Three Finger" Brown, modern-day stars Derrek Lee and Aramis Ramirez, and mid-1960s stalwarts Bill Hands and Randy Hundley. "Brown was 27 years old with a 9–13 career won-loss record," Hartig said. "The Cardinals had given up on him. Did anyone see him with six consecutive 20-win seasons while leading the Cubs to four pennants and two World Series titles? Or what about the deal with the Phillies for Fergie [for aging pitchers Bob Buhl and Larry Jackson]? Of course the Sandberg deal was among the best deals by the Cubs. Undoubtably the best deal of my Cubs era. But best all time? I'm sticking with the Cubs trading for Mordecai Brown in December 1903."

It's only natural for fans to harp on their teams' bad trades or to lament the players who got away. With the Sandberg trade (and earlier with the Jenkins trade), the Phillies fans were left to do the lamenting. "That's why I get mad when people talk about Brock for Broglio," Shaer said. "You don't hear too much about it now because a lot of the older fans are gone, but I'm telling you, I came here in 1982. Up until five or six years ago, all you heard about was Lou Brock, Brock for Broglio. It was a bad trade, and Lou Brock is a Hall of Famer. No question about it. This [Sandberg trade] should cancel that out. It's a colossal trade. It's one of the top 10 trades in baseball history. And I'm talking long term. There's a lot of other trades that yielded great results for two or three years. This yielded a Hall of Fame career.

"Why doesn't anybody—anybody—ever talk about trading Bob Buhl to the Phillies for Fergie Jenkins? That was even a greater trade. What a great trade, an even greater trade than the Sandberg trade! How come all these whining Cubs fans never talk about stealing Fergie Jenkins from the Phillies? I'll tell you something else. They never talk about stealing Randy Hundley and Bill Hands from the Giants. The Cubs have had some great trades. [The Sandberg deal] is easily in the top two."

10

The Eternal Search for a Third Baseman

Ron Santo wasted no time saying hello to the big leagues and announcing his presence.

On an early summer Sunday afternoon in Pittsburgh, on June 26, 1960, Santo stepped to the plate in the top of the second inning at Forbes Field and whistled a single past pitcher Bob Friend and into center field for his first major league hit in his first at-bat. In the fifth inning, Santo lined a three-run double to left-center to cap a six-run inning that sparked a 7–6 victory in the first game of a doubleheader, as the Chicago Cubs snapped a nine-game losing streak. In the second game, Santo went 1-for-3 with two RBIs, lifting the Cubs to a 7–5 victory and a doubleheader sweep.

Before the game Santo's call-up from the Cubs' Triple A Houston farm club was greeted with muted enthusiasm in the

Chicago Tribune: "Ron Santo, the young infielder the Cubs felt might be their outstanding rookie this season, was purchased from Houston Saturday...Santo, off to a poor start with Houston this season, is hitting [.268] with seven home runs and [32] runs batted in. [Manager Lou] Boudreau plans to station him immediately at third base."

In the next day's editions, the *Trib* reversed course and wrote a glowing review of Santo. Under a headline that said: "O, What A Lovely Day! Cubs Stun Pirates Twice, "the story read: "Ron Santo, making his major league debut, was the offensive star for the astounding Cubs, who hadn't swept a doubleheader since last September. He collected three hits in the two games and drove in five runs less than 24 hours after his arrival from Houston."

Just months after threatening to quit baseball after being sent to the minor leagues at the end of spring training, Santo was here to stay. From 1961 to 1973, he was the Cubs' Opening Day third baseman each year. That streak ended when the Cubs traded Santo to the crosstown White Sox after the '73 season. (Santo had just rejected a proposed trade to the California Angels, using the new players' right to reject a trade if they had 10 years of major league service and five with the same team. In later years, Santo jokingly referred to the right as the "Santo Clause.")

During his amazing run with the Cubs, Santo appeared in 2,102 games at third base. After he was traded, well, let's just say the Cubs used a few third basemen until they finally acquired Aramis Ramirez in the middle of the 2003 season. Ramirez and Santo put up strikingly similar numbers. In fact, each appears high on the other's list of similarity scores on Baseball Reference.

In between, the Cubs used 117 men at the hot corner. But it didn't have to be that way.

The Cubs appeared to have another long-term solution at third base beginning in 1974 with Bill Madlock, a future four-time batting champion, including twice with the Cubs. Madlock took over from Santo and started at third base for the Cubs for three straight years before being inexplicably traded away to the San Francisco Giants in a deal that netted them third baseman Steve Ontiveros and big-name outfielder Bobby Murcer.

Thus began a cold spell at the hot corner that lasted the better part of three decades with only flashes of competence and productivity in between. The reasons are myriad: poor decision making, bad drafting, and good intentions gone bad.

Steve Ontiveros, Ken Reitz, Mike Sember, Manny Trillo, Ty Waller, Ed Putman, Matt Alexander

On October 25, 1973, the Chicago Cubs made a trade that stunned some when they dealt future Hall of Fame pitcher Fergie Jenkins to the Texas Rangers for infielder Vic Harris and Bill Madlock, who had played in 21 big league games. Jenkins was an icon; he had six straight seasons of at least 20 victories for the Cubs.

One person with a contrarian take on the trade was veteran baseball writer Richard Dozer of the *Chicago Tribune*. When the trade was made, Dozer wrote: "The trade of Ferguson Jenkins came a year later than was suggested in this column, but before the second guessers have the better part of next season to castigate the Cubs for 'not getting enough' for their Canadian ace, let me be among the first to congratulate them on making what I feel is a doggone good deal.

"And from the conversations I've had with general manager John Holland, I gather that the Cubs are the benefactor of a phenomenon that is hard to explain. It can now be revealed that Holland made considerable effort to deal Jenkins during the winter meetings last November. But he was actually offered less—at a time Fergie was coming off his sixth 20-game season—than he got from the Texas Rangers this week...Leading baseball men in the country rate Madlock as one of the blue-chip rookies in the game."

Madlock finished third in Rookie of the Year voting in 1974 with a batting line of .313/.374/.442. He won the first of two consecutive batting titles in 1975 with line of .354/.402/.479. In 1976 he went .339/.412/.500 while upping his home run total from seven in 1975 to 15 in '76. There was even talk at the time that Madlock could approach the .400 mark in batting average. The Cubs had a star, and he should have been at the start of a similar run made by Ron Santo before him. But little did anyone know: the 1976 season would represent the end of the line for Madlock's Cubs career.

On February 11, 1977, Cubs general manager Bob Kennedy (a member of the infamous College of Coaches when Lou Brock was traded to the St. Louis Cardinals in 1964) announced the trade of Madlock and Rob Sperring to the San Francisco Giants for veteran outfielder Bobby Murcer, third baseman Steve Ontiveros, and minor leaguer Andrew Muhlstock. On the surface the Cubs and Madlock appeared to have come to an impasse over money. In 1976 Madlock made a reported $80,000 ($85,000 by some accounts). Coming off back-to-back batting titles, Madlock was looking for a five-year contract worth $1.5 million total. Cubs owner P.K. Wrigley reportedly ordered Kennedy to trade Madlock rather than break the $1 million barrier for a player. "Madlock wanted $1.5 million for a five-year contract," Kennedy told the *Tribune* at the time of the trade. "We can't stay in business paying that kind of money."

Oh, but they could have. They just didn't want to pay it to Madlock.

Murcer turned 31 late in the 1976 season, when he put up a line of .259/.362/.433 with 23 homers and 90 RBIs with the Giants. He made a reported $175,000 in 1976 and was looking for more money with the Cubs, who were now over a barrel. According to reports, Murcer would be getting $320,000 in each of his three seasons in Chicago (plus that amount for two more seasons after the Cubs traded him to the New York Yankees in 1979 as part of a five-year overall deal). Meanwhile in San Francisco, Madlock made $260,000 in 1977 at the start of a five-year contract worth $1.3 million.

Murcer, who never seemed happy in Chicago, had a decent 1977 with the Cubs, going .265/.355/.455 with 27 homers and 89 RBIs, but his best years were clearly behind him. He hit just nine homers in 1978 and wound up his career in 1983 with the Yankees, for whom he started as a promising young player. All the while, Jenkins went on to have productive years with the Rangers and Boston Red Sox before finishing his career with the Cubs. This would not be the first time the Cubs would compound a mistake at third base in the post-Ron Santo era.

Madlock and his agents accused the Cubs of not negotiating in good faith. Madlock said he felt the Cubs made him a scapegoat. He also rightly predicted the Cubs would pay far more for Murcer than the Giants did for him. "If [the Cubs] had negotiated, they could have signed me for much less," he said. "There were no negotiations. Whatever the Giants sign me for, the Cubs could have had me for less. They must want to pay Murcer and not me. But he's a veteran, and they won't get him cheap either."

Baseball was going through revolutionary change in the mid-1970s. The right to free agency had been granted to players via an arbitrator's decision in December 1975. Players were beginning to feel emboldened to speak up and speak out, especially Black players such as Madlock. In 1980 Madlock said this to *Chicago Tribune* columnist Robert Markus: "The way they went about it hurt me, they tried to make me a bad guy. People thought I was a militant or something. I never said anything bad about the organization."

A year later, Madlock spoke with Markus again. "If Mr. Wrigley [who died in 1977] had ever come to watch me play, I'd still have been there," he told Markus. "I got traded for all the wrong reasons. If they had gotten someone for me who could help the club, it could have been different. At the time the pay structure in baseball was changing. I was the first to ask [the Cubs] for that kind of money. Mr. Wrigley traded me, but if he had been around baseball, he would have known that the other guy would ask for even more, and they would have to pay it or look bad. But they ended up giving him more than they would have had to give to me. The Cubs always make trades because they don't like this guy's attitude instead of looking at his ability."

In 1969 the Cubs traded a promising young Black outfielder named Oscar Gamble amid whispers manager Leo Durocher and Holland didn't like Gamble's nightlife activities. No one has accused the Cubs of out-and-out racism, but many people have talked around the subject. In 1984 Cubs Hall of Famer Billy Williams spoke about it with the *Trib*'s Fred Mitchell. "They traded Bill Madlock because he dared speak out and asked for more money," Williams said in the article. "Then they turned around and paid more money to Bobby Murcer. Oscar Gamble and Madlock are two examples of good players they traded away because they didn't fit that certain mold they wanted. How can you trade a player who has won two batting titles?"

Steve Ontiveros was no Bill Madlock. In parts of four seasons with the Cubs, Ontiveros put up a line of .278/.363/.379 with 16 home runs and 150 RBIs. The Cubs released him in June of 1980 at his request so he could play in Japan. They would be in the market for yet another third baseman in 1981. On their way to getting him, they would compound another mistake.

Carmen Fanzone, Ron Cey, Ron Dunn, Mike Adams, Luis Salazar, Rodney Scott, Mick Kelleher, Rudy Meoli, Lenny Randle

Truth be told, Ken Reitz did not want to be a Cub. When Chicago Cubs general manager Bob Kennedy first tried to obtain Reitz from the St. Louis Cardinals in the fall of 1980, Reitz invoked the no-trade clause in his contract and said no to moving from St. Louis to Chicago. "I thought about it and I ain't going," he told the *Chicago Tribune*.

Kennedy and the Cubs were in a rebuilding mode, and their biggest piece of trade bait was closer Bruce Sutter, who was making $700,000 a season, a figure he won in arbitration after the Cubs offered $350,000. Kennedy wanted Reitz along with young hitting prospect named Leon Durham. There was also talk the Cubs were talking trade with the Milwaukee Brewers, offering Sutter in exchange for third baseman Jim Gantner and pitcher Mike Caldwell.

Reitz finally relented and waived his no-trade clause and he came to Chicago with Durham and a prospect named Ty Waller (who would join the Cubs' third-base parade during a short and disappointing career) in exchange for Sutter. Reitz batted .270 in 1980 with only eight errors at third base, but Kennedy talked up Durham. "Durham was the key player for me; he was especially the key player," he said. "Kenny is a quality third baseman, and frankly we didn't have a third baseman until we made this deal. The Cardinals have a chance to win the pennant with Bruce. But we have to rebuild, and he couldn't win the pennant for us."

Talk about a recurring theme.

After the trade Reitz expressed optimism about joining the Cubs. "Kennedy said he never had a guy at third he could count on every day just to write his name in the lineup and know he'd be ready to play," he said. "That's what made it easier to go."

But problems began in spring training, when Reitz had a bone chip in his knee. He decided against arthroscopic surgery and played through it. Reitz batted .192 in April, and this once popular player in St. Louis found himself being booed by the fans at Wrigley Field. For the 1981 season, he batted .215 with two homers and 28 RBIs. Under new ownership and baseball management, the Cubs released him at the end of spring training in 1982. During that spring he admitted to the *Tribune*'s Jerome Holtzman that something wasn't quite right in Chicago. "I came to the Cubs with a terrible attitude," he said. "I'll tell you when I really knew I was in trouble. It was Opening Day in Chicago. I went 3-for-3 and I had a nothing feeling about it."

As for Sutter, he helped the Cardinals win the 1982 World Series, but he was magnanimous toward the Cubs. "The Cubs made the right trade in this case," he told the *Trib*'s Steve Daley. "We weren't going anywhere with the players we had."

As a postscript, the Cubs had hoped to replace Sutter with the likes of Dick Tidrow, Bill Caudill, and a big youngster named Lee Smith. All three pitchers went on to fine careers, and Smith made the Hall of Fame. But that's a different chapter for a different book on a different day.

Fritz Connally, Steve Macko, Wayne Tyrone, Junior Kennedy, Dave Owen, Richie Hebner, Ryne Sandberg, Keith Moreland, Todd Zeile

Bob Kennedy was right that the Chicago Cubs needed to rebuild. But he would not be around to finish the job. During the summer of 1981 came the shocking news that the Tribune Company, owner of the *Chicago Tribune*, had entered into agreement to purchase the Cubs from the Wrigley family. In the fall of 1981, they hired Dallas Green away from the Philadelphia Phillies to run the Cubs' baseball operations.

On January 27, 1982, Green raided his former organization when he traded shortstop Ivan DeJesus to the Phillies for shortstop Larry Bowa and a kid infielder named Ryne Sandberg. When the Cubs released Ken Reitz at the end of spring training, they told Sandberg he would be the Opening Day third baseman.

Problem solved at third base. Except that it wasn't.

As the 1982 season wound down, Green and manager Lee Elia called Sandberg in and told him his skillset better suited him to second base than it did to third. They compared him to Bobby Grich, a standout second baseman in the American League. That part worked out okay for the Cubs. Sandberg won nine Gold Gloves at second base in what turned out to be a Hall of Fame career.

Some of the Cubs' best work at third base in the years between Ron Santo and Aramis Ramirez was done by Ron Cey, the veteran Green obtained from the Los Angeles Dodgers for Vance Lovelace and minor leaguer Dan Cataline on January 19, 1983. Even though Cey was 35, the trade turned out to be a steal for the Cubs. Known as "The Penguin," Cey was part of a famed Dodgers infield that also included Steve Garvey, Bill Russell, and Davey Lopes.

Cey played on four World Series teams with the Dodgers and he was named MVP of the 1981 World Series, when the Dodgers beat the New York Yankees. At the time of the trade to the Cubs, Cey had 228 career home runs, which ranked fourth on the Dodgers' all-time list behind Duke Snider, Gil Hodges, and Roy Campanella.

In four years with the Cubs, Cey put up a line of .254/.337/.447 with 84 home runs and 286 RBIs. He hit 24 home runs and drove in 90 in 1983. Cey helped the Cubs win the National League East in 1984, when he hit 25 home runs and had 97 RBIs. Cey's power numbers dropped to 22 home runs in 1985 and 13 in 1986. The Cubs then traded him to the Oakland A's on January 30, 1987, and the A's released him on July 15 of that year after he had played in 45 games.

Keith Moreland, obtained by Green from the Phillies in late 1981, started at third base in 1987. Vance Law, a member of the Chicago White Sox's 1983 American League West winners, started for the Cubs at third base in 1988 and '89, when the Cubs again won the National League East. Luis Salazar was the Cubs' Opening Day third baseman in 1990 before a new era was supposed to begin with a homegrown talent.

Vance Law, Steve Buechele, Dave Hansen, David Kelton, Gary Scott, Jose Nieves, Jeff Blauser

The Chicago Cubs selected Gary Scott out of Villanova in the second round of the June 1989 draft. He was going to be their third baseman of the future and he was fast-tracked to Opening Day starter in 1991 after only 150 games of minor league ball. Scott hit 10 homers in Single A in 1989 and 16 home runs (with 87 RBIs) in 1990 in Single A and Double A ball.

But in two seasons with the Cubs, Scott compiled a line of .160/.250/.240 with three home runs and 16 RBIs. The Cubs sent Scott to Triple A Iowa in both 1991 and 1992 before giving up on him and trading him to the Florida Marlins after the '92 season. Scott never played in the big leagues again.

It didn't take the Cubs long to begin hedging their bets on Scott. In July of 1992, they traded pitcher Danny Jackson to the Pittsburgh Pirates for third baseman Steve Buechele, who had carved out a decent career with the Texas Rangers from 1985 to 1991. Buechele was the Cubs' Opening Day third baseman from 1993 to 1995, but his diminishing offensive skills forced the Cubs to release him in July of '95.

The Cubs flirted with contention in 1995 under new manager Jim Riggleman and a fresh front office headed by boy wonder team president Andy MacPhail and rookie general manager Ed Lynch. Needing a third baseman during the season, Lynch and MacPhail sent pitcher Mike Morgan to the St. Louis Cardinals for veteran Todd Zeile, an impending free agent. Zeile had an odd connection with the Cubs. He was born on September 9, 1965, the day the Dodgers' Sandy Koufax tossed a perfect game against the Cubs in Los Angeles. During his introductory teleconference with the Chicago media, an unimpressed Zeile said he knew nothing of it.

The Cubs made a late charge late in the season but fell short of a wild-card berth, and Zeile left for the Philadelphia Phillies after going .227/.271/.371 with nine homers and 30 RBIs in 79 games in Chicago.

Without a bona fide everyday third baseman once again, the Cubs opened the 1996 season with utilityman Jose Hernandez at the hot corner. Leo Gomez (17 homers) saw most of the action at third base, and Dave Magadan also filled in. All the while another can't-miss prospect and his career were percolating in the minor leagues.

Kevin Orie, Brett Barberie, Leo Gomez, Dave Magadan, Bill Mueller, Miguel Cairo, Willie Greene, Chad Meyers

The Chicago Cubs selected Kevin Orie out of Indiana University in the first round of the 1993 draft. A likeable, sensitive young man, Orie shot up the Cubs' minor league system and found himself the Opening Day third baseman in 1997, when the Cubs began the season with 14 straight losses. Even so, Orie acquitted himself well, going .275/.350/.431 with eight homers and 44 RBIs, earning him Rookie of the Year votes.

Orie seemed poised to establish himself as one of the game's best young players in 1998, but a slow start at the plate seemed to damage his confidence. Orie crushed a couple of balls at Wrigley Field early in the season, but the wind held them inside the ballpark. "That started it," he said in late 2002 after coming back to the Cubs for one final go-around in the big leagues. "One thing I was trying to do was hopefully get a couple balls up and improve the power numbers. I had a good spring. I hit the ball really well in April; I just had nothing to show for it. That wind ripped the heart out of me a good four or five or six times. There were balls I couldn't hit any better. That was frustrating. I think maybe that did bother me a little bit and then I started to swing the bat not as well. That was just one more thing to throw in on the pile when I started to press a little bit. It was frustrating."

The Cubs sent him to Triple A Iowa at one point in 1998 before recalling him, but they eventually gave up, trading him to the Florida Marlins. Orie finished his baseball career with several solid seasons in the minor leagues. He bristled at being called a failed prospect or deemed as someone who had a couple bad years with Cubs. "A couple bad years when?" he asked upon his cameo return to the Cubs in 2002. "I had three bad weeks here, and that's really it. That really doesn't summarize my whole career right there as much as people want to believe that. Three bad weeks many, many years ago, I really don't even remember it."

The Cubs won the 1998 wild-card with the help of a third baseman: Gary Gaetti, whom they signed on his 40th birthday (August 19) after he had been released by the St. Louis Cardinals. Gaetti had enjoyed a distinguished career, beginning with the Minnesota Twins, and the Cubs were hoping he had a little left in the tank. He did. In 37 games with the Cubs, he had a line of .320/.397/.594 with eight home runs and 27 RBIs. One of those home runs came against the San Francisco Giants in the 163rd game of the season to help break a tie for the wild-card spot and put the Cubs into the postseason.

Gaetti signed back with the Cubs for 1999 in part because he said he liked the clubhouse culture. After games in 1998, several players lingered in the locker room to enjoy a beer, perhaps light up a cigarette, and talk baseball.

But the magic didn't last—for either Gaetti or the Cubs in 1999. The Cubs began the season 32–23 but collapsed and finished 67–95. Gaetti wound up batting only .204 with nine homers. He was released after the season and went on to play five games for the Boston Red Sox in 2000 before ending his career with 2,280 hits, 360 home runs, four Gold Gloves, and a 1987 World Series championship with the Twins.

Part of the reason the Cubs kept Gaetti was they had no third baseman in the system ready to make the jump to the big leagues. But once again, there was prospect at the lower levels who might just become the next Ron Santo and not the next Gary Scott or Orie.

David Kelton was the Cubs' second round pick of the 1998 draft. He was supposed to be part of the next wave of homegrown talent that was going to define the Cubs' future. Others in that wave included center fielder Corey Patterson, infielder Bobby Hill, first baseman Hee-Seop Choi, and catcher Jeff Goldbach. Except for brief flashes (and none for Goldbach at the big league level), none of those players were part of the long-term solution for the Cubs.

So back to the drawing board they went in September of 1999, signing Shane Andrews, who had just been released by the Montreal Expos. Andrews was a former first-round pick who hit 25 home runs for the Expos in 1998. But Andrews hit only .181 in 1999, and Montreal let him go. When the Cubs opened the 2000 season in Japan, Andrews was their third baseman. But he played in only 66 games, going .229/.329/.474 with 14 homers and 39 RBIs for a Cubs team that went 65–97. Andrews played in only seven big league games after 2000, and those came with the Red Sox in 2002. Also seeing action at third base in 2000 for the Cubs were Willie Greene, Jeff Huson, and Cole Liniak, none of whom played in the big leagues after 2000.

By the middle of the 2000 season, general manager Ed Lynch resigned. Team president Andy MacPhail took on the additional role of GM and promoted Jim Hendry to assistant GM from his role as head of scouting and player development. MacPhail wasted no time retooling the Cubs. During what was left of the 2000 season, MacPhail obtained outfielder Rondell White from the Expos. After the season ended, he said good-bye to popular first baseman Mark Grace, who went on to help the 2001 Arizona Diamondbacks win the World Series. He picked up pitchers Tom Gordon, Jason Bere, Julian Tavarez, and Jeff Fassero; infielders Matt Stairs and Ron Coomer; and catcher Todd Hundley (a move that did not pan out).

On the third-base front, MacPhail sent relief pitcher Todd Worrell to the San Francisco Giants for Bill Mueller, a switch hitter who didn't possess a whole lot of power but who could hit for average, play good defense, and provide leadership.

The team looked much improved, and with characters such as Stairs and Coomer in the clubhouse to go along with established players such as Sammy Sosa, Kerry Wood, Eric Young, and Ricky Gutierrez, it was a blast for media members to cover. The Cubs rushed out to a 21–12 start and held first place for the better part of four months before fading in August. Things might have been different for the Cubs had Mueller been able to play a full season. But on May 13, a sunny Sunday afternoon in St. Louis, Mueller chased a pop foul that was heading for the stands. He made a sliding attempt on the ball, and his knee hit the bottom of the wall underneath the protective padding. Although Mueller walked off the field with help of an athletic trainer, the injury was devastating: a broken kneecap.

Mueller had a batting line of .317/.409/.508 with five homers at the time of the injury and appeared to be on the way to a career season. He missed exactly three months, allowing the injury to heal, and the Cubs had already begun their slide by the time he came back. Coomer took over the bulk of the playing time at third base and performed admirably, but how the Cubs would have fared had Mueller not gotten hurt remains one of the great unknowns.

Although Mueller returned to the Cubs in 2002, he was not ready to start the season on time. So the Cubs went with Chris Stynes as their Opening Day third baseman. Stynes never seemed happy in Chicago and did not like dealing with the media. (He once whizzed a baseball past Bruce Miles one day in batting practice.)

Mueller managed to get back in May but was traded back to the Giants in September after the Cubs had fallen hopelessly out of the race. His career rebounded, and he won a batting title and a World Series title with the Red Sox. The 2002 season was a miserable one for the Cubs overall. They finished 67–95, and manager Don Baylor was fired in July. But bigger and better things were on the way for the Cubs—both in the standings and at third base.

Mark Bellhorn, Delino DeShields, Tyler Houston, Jeff Huson, Cole Liniak, Ramon Martinez, Lenny Harris

The Chicago Cubs opened the 2003 season with a new manager, Dusty Baker, and another starting third baseman: Mark Bellhorn.

A switch hitter and a high on-base-percentage guy, Bellhorn came to the Cubs in a trade with the Oakland A's on November 2, 2001. Bellhorn was a bright spot during a dismal 2002 season, hitting .258/.374/.512 with 27 home runs, 56 RBIs, and an OPS-plus of 133 (100 is league average). But he could not duplicate his success of 2002 in 2003. He batted .200 with one homer in March/April and .235 with one homer in May.

That typified the first two-thirds of the season, which began well enough for the Cubs with a 15–2 victory against the New York Mets at frigid Shea Stadium. Center fielder Corey Patterson set the tone with two home runs and seven RBIs. Kerry Wood picked up the victory, and expectations were high with a rotation fronted by Wood that included Mark Prior, Carlos Zambrano, and Matt Clement.

Things were looking up. But even though the Cubs went all the way to Game Seven of the National League Championship Series, much of the season was one of fits and starts. After going 15–12 in March/April and in May, the Cubs were 12–15 in June and 12–14 in July. They also had to withstand the controversy of Sammy Sosa getting caught with a corked bat and being suspended in early June.

Third base was a problem. Bellhorn wasn't hitting, and on July 6, Patterson suffered a season-ending knee injury while running to first base. Patterson's once-promising season ended with him having a line of .298/.329/.511 with 13 home runs, 55 RBIs, and 16 stolen bases. The Cubs did call up prospect David Kelton in June, but he went just 2-for-12 in 10 games before being sent back to the minor leagues. He came back to the Cubs for eight games in 2004, when he was 1-for-10. That was the end of his major league career—another Cubs third base prospect washing out too soon.

The Cubs were in trouble at two positions: third base and center field. They already had given up on Bellhorn, trading him to the Colorado Rockies on June 20. (Bellhorn would go on to win a world championship with the Boston Red Sox in 2004.) The Cubs were using the likes of utilitymen Jose Hernandez, Ramon Martinez, and Lenny Harris at third base. In center field they were trotting out the likes of Hernandez, Tom Goodwin, and Trent Hubbard.

As the All-Star break approached, Hendry was looking all over for help at both center field and third base. During the break it looked like he might have a deal for Rockies center fielder Jeromy Burnitz (whom Hendry would acquire in 2005 to replace Sosa), but nothing came of it. Then on July 23, Hendry took care of both positions in one fell swoop. In what has to go down as one of the best trades in the history of the Cubs, Hendry sent minor league pitcher Matt Bruback, Hernandez, and a player to be named later, who turned out to be infield prospect Bobby Hill, to the Pittsburgh Pirates for third baseman Aramis Ramirez and center fielder Kenny Lofton. "It was my first year as GM, and we knew we didn't have a third baseman,"

Hendry recalled in 2022. "If you remember at the [2002] winter meetings, we thought we were trading for Joe Randa with the Royals. We kept trying during the year. We liked Aramis' talent, and he was young. He was getting a little bit of the rap that he was not playing hard and things like that when we got him from Pittsburgh. We got real lucky. [Cubs scout] Kenny Kravec really liked him when he scouted him for me before the trade.

"When Patterson went down, we worked really hard with [Pirates general manager] Dave Littlefield to try to get both [Ramirez and Lofton] in the same deal. I remember talking not only to Kenny Kravec, but to Dusty that he thought, too, that Ramirez, and a change of scenery and putting him on a contending team would really help. And that's exactly what happened. He became a guy that was right up there with the best in the league in knocking in runs. He loved hitting with men on base. He loved when the games were close. He wasn't afraid. He became a great RBI guy. He was more than adequate at third, too. It was good fortune. I'd not be telling the truth if I said we didn't try to get other guys before him. But as fate would have it, it did turn out to be a great trade. Kenny Lofton was exactly what we needed, too, when Patterson went down with the knee injury."

The deal was a heist. For very little, Hendry got an established center fielder and spark plug in Lofton and a budding star in the power-hitting Ramirez. At the time of the deal, Ramirez was batting .280/.330/.448 with 12 homers and 67 RBIs for the Pirates. His RBI total was more than any Cubs player at the time. He had 18 homers and 71 RBIs in 2002 and 34 homers and 112 RBIs in 2001. The knocks against him were that he was an indifferent fielder and someone who did not always hustle. Ramirez worked on his fielding with the Cubs and became a solid third baseman even as the charges of not hustling dogged him, unfairly, for almost all of his career.

At the end of the day's play on July 23, the Cubs were 50–50 and spinning their wheels. They went on to finish 88–74 (19–8 in September) with Ramirez and Lofton playing key roles. After being traded to the Cubs, Ramirez hit 15 home runs and drove in 39. Lofton batted .327 with three homers, 20 RBIs, and 12 stolen bases, giving the Cubs a bona fide threat out of the leadoff spot. The Cubs fell short of the World Series in 2003, and Lofton signed with the New York Yankees in the offseason. He was a short-term fix anyway. Ramirez was keeper, and the Cubs managed to keep him through the 2011 season.

Here is how his Cubs numbers compare to those of Ron Santo, the gold standard of Cubs third basemen:

Santo: 14 seasons, .279/.366/.472, 337 home runs, 1,290 RBIs, 128 OPS-plus (100 is league average), 72.1 WAR (wins above replacement)

Ramirez: Nine seasons, .294/.356/.531, 239 home runs, 806 RBIs, 126 OPS-plus, 24.1 WAR.

On Santo's similarity scores on Baseball Reference, Ramirez is first. On Ramirez's similarity scores, Santo ranks second. Each shares top 10 similarity scores with Scott Rolen and Gary Gaetti.

Santo was the better defender, having won five Gold Gloves and making nine All-Star teams. Ramirez never won a Gold Glove, but he made three All-Star teams, including two while on the Cubs. He committed 33 errors in 2003 between Pittsburgh and Chicago but made only 10 in 2004 and never again approached 33.

Ramirez's perceived lack of hustle oftentimes was born of leg injuries that bothered him throughout his career. He was told by management and managers to take it easy on his legs because the Cubs needed his bat in the lineup. "As you know, I'm an Aramis fan," Hendry said. "I do believe that he had great way of slowing the game down, especially with a bat in his hand.

I never thought he dogged it. The bigger the game in a pennant race, you wanted him on your side all the time. He made the plays [in the field], too. If you were going to be any way critical at all, not critical, but the years we were out of it, he would take a day or two off here or there that we wouldn't have taken if we were in it. But I think that was a lower-body situation that he did have trouble with. I got no problem at all. When you needed him to be there in a big game, he went to the post all the time."

Although the sabermetrics community scoffs at the notion that there are clutch hitters, Ramirez often took pride in his ability to drive in big runs. "That's what I'm paid to do," he invariably said when asked about the subject.

Ramirez hit walk-off home runs in 2007 and 2008 to help the Cubs to division titles in both years. On the Cubs' all-time leaderboard, he ranks third in slugging percentage, fifth in OPS, and seventh in home runs. He's a worthy successor to Santo's legacy and somehow he remains an underappreciated Cub—perhaps because of some of the perceived knocks against him.

In 2015, while finishing his career with the Pirates, he reflected on his time with the Cubs in an interview with the *Daily Herald*. "I played there eight-plus years," he said. "I can't regret a bit. If I had to do it again, I would. We made the playoffs three times. I thought I did my job every single year there, just a real fun time. The goal for every single baseball player, for every manager, is to be in the World Series. We didn't achieve that. We were close a few times. I thought in '08 we had a great team, and we didn't do it. Sometimes it doesn't work the way you expect."

Like most players while they're still playing, Ramirez was reluctant to talk about his legacy in the game. "I don't know, man, I really don't know," he said. "Everybody has a different look. They look at players differently. They look at things differently. I'm just a guy who comes and plays every single day. I've been a big RBI guy my whole career, so that's probably how they're going to remember me."

Hendry, however, was glad to weigh in. "His legacy should be that he was part of a change with us that losing was no longer considered okay," he said. "He added to that right away in '03, and that continued. I remember when his contract the first time was up, guys like Derrek Lee calling me and saying, 'Jim, we've got to keep him, man. He's part of what we're doing.' Let's face it: For the most part from '03 to '09, we had a fighting chance most of the time, and I think his legacy would be that he produced when it counted, which is always a judge for me of hitters. You can go by numbers all you want, but who does it in the clutch? Who does it with men on base? Who does it late in the game? He was right up there with some of the best we've had. He was always an RBI guy. I always had great dealings with him. I signed him to two different contracts. He was fair and honest with me and appreciative and the whole deal. I wouldn't say a bad word about him. He did me nothing but right in the years we were there and had a fighting chance."

Postscript: Ramirez signed with the Milwaukee Brewers after the 2011 season. The Cubs thought they had their next long-term third baseman in 2013 when they took Kris Bryant with the second overall pick in the draft. Bryant came up in April of 2015 and went on to win the Rookie of the Year award. In 2016 Bryant won the Most Valuable Player award in helping the Cubs to their first World Series title since 1908. Although drafted as a third baseman, Bryant played all over the diamond for the Cubs. His tenure with the Cubs ended as part of a roster purge in 2021. Where will the Cubs' next great third baseman come from and when will he get here? Stay tuned.

11

The Jake Arrieta Trade

ONE OF THE BEST PITCHERS IN CHICAGO CUBS HISTORY—
at least for a short period of time—was anything but great
before he was traded to the North Side of Chicago. Jacob Joseph
Arrieta was a member of the Baltimore Orioles, beginning his
Major League Baseball career in 2010. But two short years later,
his career was directionless. Though he was their Opening Day
starter in his final full season with the Orioles, he was pitching
like he belonged in the minors.

A fifth-round pick from TCU in 2007, Arrieta worked his
way up through Baltimore's system and looked ready for the
major leagues by the time 2010 rolled around. His 1.85 ERA
in his final year in the minors earned him a call-up. Two years
later, he was a mess.

Arrieta was 3–9 with a 6.20 ERA in 2012. He was ripe to be traded. "I didn't connect with my pitching coach," Arrieta said after finding success in Chicago. "They wanted to change my pitching style."

The Orioles changed pitching coaches not long after Arrieta made it to the big leagues. His delivery was a bit unique, as he threw across his body instead of stepping and then throwing in a straight line to his catcher. The crossfire motion was different, and it's what made him special. But he claims the Orioles tried to change him. "There were so many things in Baltimore not many people know about," Arrieta told *Sports Illustrated*. "I had struggles with my pitching coach [Rick Adair]. A lot of guys did. Three or four guys…were just really uncomfortable in their own skins at the time, trying to be the guys they weren't. You can attest how difficult it is to try to reinvent your mechanics against the best competition in the world."

Arrieta felt he had gotten to the majors pitching one way and then was being asked to do it differently. He was confused, and his career was going in the wrong direction—until the Cubs stepped in. The team had already identified Arrieta as a buy-low candidate. Every organization in the league looks for those kinds of bargains, where untapped potential is lying in wait. And the Cubs, in that moment, could afford a project. They weren't necessarily in a must-win mode, which usually entails trading prospects for proven commodities. This was the opposite situation. Soon enough, the Cubs would enter a winning phase where deals like the one for Arrieta wouldn't make sense, but in 2013 they had some veteran commodities of value and identified the then-27 year old as a pitcher with untapped potential. As happens every summer, contending teams looking to add veteran help call organizations willing to give them up.

Baltimore needed starting pitching, and Orioles general manager Dan Duquette contacted the Cubs.

At the time the Cubs employed 30-year-old right-hander Scott Feldman, who was only three years older than Arrieta. It underscored the risk the Cubs were taking, which of course seems silly now. But in 2013 it was Feldman who was established, while Arrieta—just a couple years away from hitting 30 himself—hadn't done much of anything in the big leagues.

Feldman was 7–6 with a 3.46 ERA in 15 starts for the Cubs through June of 2013. He was pitching well, giving up just 79 hits in 91 innings, but the Cubs were going nowhere that season, and Feldman was due to be a free agent after the year was over. The team made sure to max out on those kinds of players during a rebuilding stage in the middle of that decade. Why lose a guy to free agency for nothing when you can get with Arrieta's talent for him? Of course, it's not as simple as that. "We felt Arrieta had a good arm, and there was some upside, but, honestly, no one knew what he would turn into," Cubs president of baseball operations at the time Theo Epstein said.

So Feldman for Arrieta seemed like a fairly straightforward deal—except the Cubs weren't done. Epstein credits general manager Jed Hoyer for extracting more out of Baltimore. "Jed kept on pounding the table that we could get a throw-in," Epstein said. "It had to be this guy named Pedro Strop, even though he had like an 11.00 ERA the year before with the Orioles and was seemingly lost at the time as a pitcher. Jed kept pounding the table, saying, 'Not only can we can we get more, but he's the right guy.'"

Strop was also a bit older (28) for a pitcher who hadn't completely established himself. Baltimore was his second stop in the majors after having pitched for the Texas Rangers for a couple of seasons. In 2012 he compiled a 2.44 ERA in 70 games but in 2013—the year Epstein referenced—it ballooned to 7.25 in his first 29 games. Like Arrieta, he seemed ripe for the taking. Strop didn't have the issues with the pitching coach with the Orioles in the same way that Arrieta did, but he struggled nonetheless. "I don't know what happened in Baltimore," Strop said. "Maybe a change of scenery was good. I'm so happy they made the deal."

The Cubs added catcher Steve Clevenger to the trade in what would end up being one of the most lopsided deals in team history: a backup catcher and a free-agent-to-be for a future Cy Young winner and a solid back-end reliever. On July 2, 2013, the Cubs made the trade with Baltimore, never knowing at the time how one-sided it would turn out to be. "That's one I always think back on because there's no doubt if it weren't for Jed being insistent on that and driving that, we would not have gotten Stropy in the deal—let alone maybe complete the deal—and then without Jake Arrieta, all of the history here is different," Epstein said.

Here is how the deal was analyzed in *The Baltimore Sun* by various reporters and columnists.

Dan Connolly, baseball reporter: "Feldman pitched for [Orioles manager Buck] Showalter in Texas, and the manager loves the guy's attitude. But it's not just about team morale. Feldman has a 3.46 ERA in 15 starts for the Cubs this year and has made nine postseason appearances as a reliever (3.29 ERA). Steve Clevenger is a Mount St. Joe guy that will go to Triple A Norfolk and can be used as a catcher and bat off the bench if needed in Baltimore. The risk here is giving up two high-ceiling arms in Jake Arrieta and Pedro Strop. But the Orioles love Feldman and figure it's worth the risk."

Peter Schmuck, columnist: "For the second year in a row, Dan Duquette has pulled off a significant deal for a veteran starting pitcher, which is never an easy thing to do. The Orioles may end up regretting the loss of Arrieta, but it was starting to look like he wasn't going to bloom here."

Childs Walker, sports enterprise reporter: "The Orioles made a sharp move acquiring Scott Feldman ahead of the deadline. This is a classic case of a contender trading uncertain assets to address a current problem. Jake Arrieta has the talent to make the deal look bad some day. But the Orioles can't count on him to figure it out in the next three months, and they have a real chance to make a run this year. To do that, they need a more trustworthy rotation. They know it. Everyone knows it. And Dan Duquette has been right more often than not in targeting these kinds of players. He got the guy they needed without giving up an elite prospect."

David Selig, baseball editor: "Feldman is having a good year for the Cubs, but he's 46–50 for his career with a 4.66 ERA, so he's not coming here to be an ace. The fact that Strop was out of minor league options obviously is a big factor in the Orioles trading him. He still has potential as a late-inning reliever and he won't be pitching in a pennant race in Chicago in the near future, so they can better afford to hold him on the big league roster. It's also a better bet that Jake Arrieta will succeed in the National League than pitching in the AL East at Camden Yards."

Only Selig combined some doubt about acquiring Feldman with an understanding of what the Orioles were giving up, but most *were* clear, Baltimore was saying good-bye to two high-end arms. Now it was up to Cubs coaches—and the players themselves—to ensure that the trade was a good one for Chicago.

Incidentally, Feldman pitched okay for the Orioles for the rest of that season before signing with the Houston Astros. His ancillary stats were nearly identical with Baltimore as they were with Chicago, but his ERA rose from 3.46 in 15 starts with the Cubs to 4.27 in 15 starts with the Orioles. Meanwhile, Arrieta flashed signs of his talent in his first few outings for the Cubs in 2013. He gave up just four hits in his first 13 innings with his new team, but walks plagued him over the course of those first few months. "My mechanics were nowhere near locked in," he said at the time. "I was learning myself all over again."

Arrieta walked 14 batters in his first four starts heading into the final month of the season. In September he never walked more than three in a start. Cubs pitching coach Chris Bosio was just getting to know Arrieta and vice versa. "Just try to communicate with them," Bosio told NBC Sports Chicago. "These guys know we care about them. But it's important talking to them about what they want to do, what they're comfortable with, and then work on cans and can'ts."

Said Arrieta: "I could tell Bosio was different. He was listening to me. I began to get back to what made me get to the big leagues in the first place. Chicago let me do that."

Arrieta, of course, was talking about that crossfire delivery, nearly unique to him. Bosio understood it and didn't hold his new pitcher back. By the next season (2014), things began to take off. "I told him, 'Be yourself,'" Bosio stated at the time. "We'll make adjustments along the way, but your style is what got you here."

The numbers improved greatly in 2014 as Arrieta became nearly unhittable at times, lining up on the third-base side of the rubber and throwing across his body. When his mechanics were flawless, the speed and movement of his pitches—especially his cutter, which moved like a slider—made him one of the toughest pitchers to hit. By 2015 he had mastered his craft, and opposing batters hit just .185 off him—the lowest in baseball. "I was able to not hold anything back or feel like I was judged," Arrieta told *Sports Illustrated*. "People had lost faith in me in Baltimore and rightfully so. I knew that was not the guy I was. [Now] I was letting it out as hard as I could in a controlled way. I was across my body. I felt strong. I felt explosive."

Bosio added: "We try to let these guys do their thing and be themselves. Pedro Strop, for example, 'Where do you feel comfortable on the mound?' Same thing with Jake."

About two years after making the trade, it was looking like a winner for the Cubs, but to go down in history, Arrieta became otherworldly. That occurred in the second half of 2015. It's when everything came together for the eventual Cy Young winner. "I've never seen anything like that," teammate Jon Lester said. "Even as a pitcher, I'm in awe of what he can do with a baseball."

Arrieta made 15 starts after the All-Star break in 2015, producing a minuscule 0.75 ERA. He went 12–1, giving up just 55 hits in 107.1 innings pitched. He also threw the first of his two no-hitters. It's arguably considered the best second half by a pitcher in the history of the game, rivaling the great Bob Gibson from 1968. "I don't want to sound like an [ass] about it, but I don't know if that second half will ever be broken," Arrieta told *Sports Illustrated*. "It's hard to put into words. Being in the same sentence as Bob Gibson, that's incredible."

Bosio added: "We'll never see something like that again. He was pure magic that second half."

Arrieta alone probably solidifies the trade in Cubs lore, but Strop's performance over his career with the Cubs simply adds to the mystique of it all. Strop pitched in parts of nine different seasons for the Cubs, also realizing his potential just as the team was blossoming. From 2013 to 2018, he never compiled an ERA higher than 2.91 while performing in various roles. One year he was a set-up man; the next he helped close games. In all, Strop had 29 saves for the Cubs while helping them reach the playoffs multiple times and win one championship. "Some people forget about Strop because Arrieta was so good," Hoyer said. "But he was just as important to our bullpen as Arrieta was to our starting staff."

Arrieta threw his second no-hitter in 2016 as his team won the World Series. By then, Feldman was beginning to wind down his career—2017 would be his last season—while Clevenger would be out of baseball that same year. The trade looked better and better as time passed on. "I'm not sure we could ever have imagined getting both those guys in one deal," Bosio said. "They deserve all the credit. They wanted to be the best pitchers they possibly could be, and we just let them be themselves. Sometimes that's all it takes."

PART 4

THE LOVABLE LOSERS

12
The 1969 Season

EVERYTHING WAS GOING THE CHICAGO CUBS' WAY ON THE
beautiful summer afternoon of August 19, 1969. Even the wind
was blowing in the Cubs' favor. The breeze was described as a
16-mph nor'easter, coming over the center-field wall and pro-
viding cooling breeze on a lovely sunny day. On that August
afternoon, left-hander Ken Holtzman tossed a no-hitter against
the Atlanta Braves. He did so without recording a single strikeout. The Cubs' only runs in a 3–0 victory came in the first
inning on a three-run homer by Ron Santo off knuckleballer
Phil Niekro in a confrontation of future Hall of Famers.

And about that wind? It knocked down what looked to be
a surefire home run off the bat of Henry Aaron in the seventh
inning. Cubs announcer Jack Brickhouse thought the ball was
long gone. But left fielder Billy Williams stayed with it and
caught it in "the well," or the curve in the wall where the left-
field bleachers bordered a catwalk down the line. "That's well

hit," Brickhouse said. "And there, I believe, goes the no-hitter. Caught! Caught by Williams! Hoo boy!"

Holtzman thought the potential no-no was a no-go at that point, too. "I thought it was gone, even with the wind blowing in," Holtzman told reporters after the game. "Without the wind that ball would have landed in Evanston."

The victory kept the Cubs eight games on top in the new National League East, one game off their biggest cushion of the season at nine games, which was last achieved on August 16. Sent into delirium again by their beloved Cubs, the crowd of 41,033 went home happy again. There was no stopping these Cubs, who ended the day with a record of 77–45.

Except that there was.

After Holtzman's no-hitter, the Cubs went 15–25, while the upstart New York Mets went 33–11 to breeze past the Cubs and finish 100–62, eight games ahead of the Cubs, who seemed to run out of gas physically, mentally, and emotionally. It was a collapse of epic proportions, the low point of which may have come on September 9 at Shea Stadium in New York, where a black cat infamously crossed the path of Santo while he waited in the on-deck circle.

Such failure would be ignominious in most cities with most sports teams. But instead of being shamed or shunned, the 1969 Cubs have been saluted and celebrated over the ensuing decades to the amusement, bemusement, and even the dismay of some. "I still can't believe people here respect losing that much," former team president Dallas Green told the *Chicago Tribune* in 1989. Shortly after the Tribune Co. bought the Cubs from the Wrigley family in 1981, it brought in Green, whose slogan of "Building a New Tradition" was meant to rid the Cubs of their image as "Lovable Losers," a term wholly embodied by the 1969 team.

Nevertheless, the 1969 Cubs will always hold a special place in the hearts of Cubs fans. During his final Cubs convention in January 1998, Brickhouse, whose excited calls on TV provided the soundtrack of the summer of 1969 (and many others), hosted a session on the '69 Cubs and had to calm the crowd down at the beginning. "Now if you all settle down, we can talk to these guys and find out just what the hell happened," he said as he pointed toward the panel of '69 Cubs members.

The question that remains is why. Why does a team, which in the end didn't come close to gaining the postseason, hold such a special place in the hearts of Cubs fans? "One thing is we stayed together for so many years," Williams said. "When you look at those fun years, and we happened to be close in 1969, we made a lot of people happy. From that point on, every time we were in the city, every time we would walk around the city, a lot of people would come up to me and say, 'That was so much fun in the '60s.' Another thing, too, is that we couldn't afford two homes. We had to live in one place, and that one place was in Chicago."

The story of the 1969 Cubs and how they became so beloved begins well before that magical summer. After winning the National League pennant and losing the World Series in 1945, the Cubs went into a postwar funk, and that's putting it mildly. After finishing third in the eight-team NL in 1946, the Cubs finished in what was called the second division (bottom half of the standings) every season from 1947 to 1966. Included were five last-place finishes.

Without a doubt the low point in this run of incompetence was the "College of Coaches" era from 1961 to 1965, when the Cubs went with rotating head coaches instead of a manager, as other coaches rotated up and back from the minor leagues. Confusion reigned, as befuddled players listened to sometimes conflicting sets of instructions on how to play the game. One such player who no doubt was hurt by the College of Coaches was an athletically-gifted outfielder named Lou Brock. Was Brock a power hitter, a base stealer, a slap hitter? He heard all the advice, and the Cubs gave up on him on June 15, 1964, when they traded him to the St. Louis Cardinals for pitcher Ernie Broglio. The trade was initially praised in the Chicago media. The Cubs were getting a proven pitcher for a player who looked like he may never pan out.

But Broglio was damaged goods with a sore arm (in the days before a full medical report would be provided to the team acquiring him), and Brock went on to a Hall of Fame career, helping the Cardinals win three pennants and two World Series championships. The College of Coaches madness stopped after an eighth-place finish in 1965. Late that year, the Cubs hired firebrand Leo Durocher, who let it be known that he was coming to Chicago to be the manager and not the head coach. He also proclaimed that the Cubs were not an eighth-place ballclub.

Durocher was right. The Cubs finished 10th in his first season with a record of 59–103.

But there was hope. The Cubs still had Hall of Famer Ernie Banks (of whom Durocher was intensely jealous), and future Hall of Famers Santo and Williams were in their primes. Before the 1966 season, general manager John Holland made a shrewd trade with the San Francisco Giants, obtaining pitcher Bill Hands and catcher Randy Hundley. Early in the miserable 1966 season, Holland pried a young pitcher named Ferguson Jenkins from the Philadelphia Phillies. Jenkins was up and coming, but no one knew then he would be a Hall of Famer, too. And the Cubs were developing a double-play combination of Don Kessinger at shortstop and Glenn Beckert at second base. Beckert might not have been there at all if not for the tragic death of Ken Hubbs in a plane crash in February of 1964. That leads one to wonder how the 1969 Cubs may have fared had they kept Brock and had Hubbs not been killed.

Things began coming together in 1967. When the Cubs beat the Cincinnati Reds 4–1 at Wrigley Field on Sunday, July 2, to garner a share of first place, fans would not leave the ballpark until the scoreboard crew placed the Cubs flag atop the National League standings.

The powerhouse Cardinals were too much for the Cubs in 1967, as they were in 1968, cruising to back-to-back National League pennants and a world championship in '67. But a phenomenon was born on the North Side, and there was a changing of the guard in Chicago baseball. From 1951 to 1967, the South Side White Sox were contenders most years and they won the American League pennant in 1959, ending a 40-year drought. But the Sox collapsed in 1968, losing their first 10 games of the season, setting off a three-year period of darkness that saw them go 68–94 in 1969 and 56–106 in 1970.

On top of that, the White Sox left WGN-TV after the 1967 season for the short-term cash grab from Chicago's new UHF channel, WFLD Channel 32, which not all viewers could receive or receive clearly. Before 1968 WGN televised all Cubs home games (played in the daytime) and a handful of night, road games. The Sox had their home day games televised along with select home night games and a few road games. The Cubs and Sox had a kind of gentlemen's agreement not to televise against each other, but once the Sox left for Channel 32, Cubs owner P.K. Wrigley gave WGN a far-below-market-value deal to televise the vast majority of their games.

The Cubs got off to an 11–1 start in 1969 and, during the height of the Vietnam War and general unrest in the country, the Cubs provided welcome respite from everyday trouble and

THE FRANCHISE: CHICAGO CUBS

strife. Every day was a party at Wrigley Field as the Cubs moved closer to a goal that had eluded them since 1945. In left field the original Bleacher Bums donned their yellow hard hats and cheered the Cubs' every move, often egged on from the bullpen by pitcher Dick Selma.

"If you lived in Chicago and were at least seven years old in 1967, you couldn't help but follow the 'The Happening' at Clark and Addison, led by the 'Original Left Field Bleacher Bums' with their yellow helmets, bed sheets with blue spray-painted wacky slogans, and the Mad Bugler leading cheers while standing on the top of the wall above the 368' sign," said Mike Murphy, the Mad Bugler who later went on to fame as a Chicago sports talk radio personality. "All four Chicago newspapers, all the radio stations, all the TV stations covered the blossoming story. It also being 'The Flower Power Summer of Love' in the United States was just a coincidence. Or was it? The Cubs suddenly winning games— often in dramatic fashion—consumed the city [well, except for the White Sox fans] in 1967, '68, and '69. Sure, winning helps… but—not unlike the 1985 Super Bowl Bears—most all of the Cubs players were famously charismatic. And the cantankerous baseball legend Leo 'The Lip' Durocher as Cubs manager didn't hurt the stranger-than-truth buzz of the story either. Even non-fans soon knew the names of all the players. Especially the young future Hall of Famers—Fergie Jenkins, Ron Santo, Billy Williams—all emerging into full-blown star status careers simultaneously."

Local businesses got involved, and it wasn't unusual to see a Cubs player appearing in TV commercials. "Go to the local Jewel food store in the summer of '69 and you would see displays of white Cubs coffee cups for sale," Murphy said. "One cup had the embossed blue autographs of the infielders, one with the outfielders, one with the starting pitchers and catcher, and even one with all the bullpen guys. 'Collect all four Cubs coffee cups!' Soon, the

168

Cubs were being seen coast to coast on the Saturday NBC *Game of the Week* with Curt Gowdy and Tony Kubek. Understand the Cubs had *not* been on the national game in years—if ever!"

The fun lasted until September. The Cubs entered the month four-and-a-half games ahead of the Mets but went 8–17 (1–1 in October) while the Mets streaked away with a September record of 23–7 after going 21–10 in August. The Cubs lost eight straight from September 3–11, including a two-game sweep at the hands of the Mets in New York, when the black cat crossed their paths. Until the Cubs won the World Series in 2016, many fans believed in the "Curse of the Billy Goat," when a local tavern owner was denied entrance to Wrigley Field for the 1945 World Series because he had a goat in tow. Now, there was a black cat.

Williams, though, said the black cat had nothing at all to do with the Cubs' collapse. "Hell, no," he said emphatically. "The Mets, they played good baseball. I don't know how many games they won [down the stretch], but it was outrageous. They played like .700 baseball [.767 in September]. It was just a coincidence. I think that all the people over the years with what had been happening from that day on, the Bartman thing, the other stuff, they thought about that. When those things happened, that ran through their minds, the black cat. But I don't think the players thought anything of it until afterward. That night it was just a black cat on the field."

That cat was the cause of some amusement—even if it was gallows humor. "The most I can say about the black cat is that it scared the shit out of Ronnie," Williams said with a laugh. "I don't know how the cat got in there unless somebody brought the cat and just threw him in there. I remember seeing a picture of it, and Leo was on the bench. Guys were looking at Santo and looking around. We didn't think anything of it."

There were other bumps along the road—in the form of controversy—during the Cubs' version of the Summer of Love, but none proved fatal, even if there were long-term ramifications. On the afternoon of July 8 at Shea Stadium, Jenkins and the Cubs held a 3–1 lead as the upstart Mets came to bat in the bottom of the ninth. Light-hitting Ken Boswell led off and hit a fly ball into short center field.

Playing center field for the Cubs was rookie Don Young (who had a cup of coffee with the team in 1965). Young misread the flight of Boswell's ball. He took a couple of steps backward before coming in. It was too late. Boswell raced to second base for a double. One out later, the dangerous Donn Clendenon hit a drive to deep left-center field. Young appeared to have made the catch, but the ball fell out of his glove as he crashed into the wall. Boswell stopped at third base, and Clendenon went to second. The next batter, Cleon Jones, drove in both runners with a single. An intentional walk to Art Shamsky and a ground-out by Wayne Garrett put runners on second and third with two outs and the game tied at 3–3. Veteran Ed Kranepool then punched a single to left to give the Mets a stunning victory.

Both Durocher and Santo took after Young verbally. "My three year old could have caught those balls," said Durocher, as recounted in Ron Rapoport's book about Banks, *Let's Play Two*.

Santo blamed Young for "thinking of himself" and having his head down after a bad day at the plate. "He's out there thinking about how he didn't [hit] anything out of the infield and forgot that we had a 3–1 lead and were going to win the game. He had a bad day at the bat, so he's got his head down. He's worrying about his batting average and not the team. All right, he can keep his head down and he can keep right on going out of sight for all I care. We don't need that kind of thing."

That was the 1969 version of throwing a teammate under the bus, and if there is a 1969 version of something "going viral," Santo touched it off. Young, who did not play in the major leagues after 1969, was disconsolate and in disbelief. Santo felt the backlash and called the Chicago beat writers to his hotel room the next morning to say he had apologized to Young.

On July 9, Mets ace and rising star Tom Seaver nearly pitched a perfect game against the Cubs. A one-out single in the ninth inning by rookie Jim Qualls ended Seaver's no-hitter and attempt at perfection. A Cubs five-game losing streak ended the next day, and their lead in the division was at four-and-a-half games after the series in New York, but they never seemed to recover from the Santo–Young contretemps.

Santo also angered many opponents with his habit of running down the left-field line toward the Cubs' clubhouse, jumping up, and clicking his heels after home victories. The heel-clicking had the full blessing of Durocher, but it angered many players on other teams. Unlike today, showboating was severely frowned upon in those old-school days. Even though the Cubs were a romantic story in Chicago in '69, players on other teams were rooting for the Mets to overtake them and win the National League East.

Throughout much of his playing career, Santo lagged in popularity among fans to Banks and Williams. He also could be the target of Wrigley Field boo birds. It wasn't until he became a Cubs radio analyst years later that he became a fully beloved figure among Cubs fans, who identified with the way he wore his heart on his sleeve during the broadcasts.

Durocher caused his own problems and nearly lost his job later in the month when he left a game at Wrigley Field early, ostensibly with an illness. It turns out he flew in a private plane to Eagle River, Wisconsin, for a parents' weekend at Camp

Ojibwa, where the son of his wife, Lynne Goldblatt, was an attendee. When word of that got out—as news of those sorts of things invariably do, even in 1969—Cubs owner P.K. Wrigley found it difficult not to fire his manager. Durocher blamed the writers, and his relationship with them gradually deteriorated.

Again, the Cubs weathered a tempest. "As for distractions there were plenty," said research historian Ed Hartig. "Durocher leaving the team on a couple occasions, the Don Young game, all the personal appearances, the team recording an album, Santo clicking his heals, Leo's feud with the press. But I don't think the distraction was as much of a factor as claimed. Actually, the Cubs improved their place in the standings after some of the distractions, including the Don Young game. Plus, with all the media attention in New York, wouldn't the distraction have been even greater in New York than Chicago?"

The reasons for the Cubs' late-season collapse are myriad: a full schedule of day games at Wrigley Field sapped their energy, the Mets simply got hot, and the widely-held belief that Durocher wore out his regulars while Mets manager Gil Hodges used his full roster. "We didn't tire out, but we stopped hitting. I know that," Williams said. "The Mets just played magnificent baseball. Leo would come into the clubhouse and say, Kess [Don Kessinger], are you tired?' And Kess would say, 'Noooooooooo.'"

Years later, Hundley, who was a workhorse for Durocher in his early years as a Cub, playing 149 games in 1966, 152 in 1967, 160 in 1968, and 151 in 1969, told the *Chicago Tribune* that he enjoyed the schedule of all days games at home and that it should have been an advantage for the Cubs to use against their opponents. "It was a 9-to-5 job," he told the *Trib* in 1998. "You go to the park, you play, you go home and have dinner and do it again the next day. I loved it. There was some semblance to a regular lifestyle."

Hartig, though, pointed out several differences in the way Durocher and Hodges managed their respective teams and how it could have played into the final result. "Cubs starters at seven of eight field positions played at minimum the equivalent 16 more games [144 innings] than their Mets counterpart," Hartig said. "And that's at least. In most cases it was significantly worse. Randy Hundley caught 1,290⅓ innings for the Cubs. Jerry Grote, the Mets' starting catcher, caught only 918⅔ innings. That's equivalent to 41 more games. And it's only 41 games because Hundley was hospitalized and couldn't play during a stretch in August."

Hartig cited other stats:

- First base: The Cubs' 38-year-old Banks played 43 games more than Kranepool.
- Second base: Beckert played 29 games more than Boswell.
- Third base: Santo played 36 games more than Garrett.
- Shortstop: Kessinger played 35 games more than Bud Harrelson.
- Left field: Williams played 26 games more than Jones.

Now, in fairness to Durocher, the Cubs played two exhibition games in August, something that would be utterly unthinkable today. After playing at San Diego on August 13, the Cubs flew to Tacoma, Washington, to play their Triple A affiliate on August 14. Just four days later, they played the White Sox in the annual Boys Benefit Game at Comiskey Park. Durocher had talked of resting most of his regulars for those two meaningless games, but he relented under public and media pressure in both Tacoma and Chicago. In the August 18 edition of the *Chicago Tribune*, columnist Robert Markus wrote: "A few weeks back, Leo reached the height of selfishness, even for Leo., when he announced that six Cubs regulars, the heart of the team, would not make an appearance in tonight's annual Cubs–Sox game for the benefit of boys baseball in Chicago."

That was the kind of sniping that began to intensify with the Chicago media toward Durocher, who relented and played his regulars at least for parts of the exhibition games. Banks and Santo homered in the game at Tacoma. Banks and Williams hit homers against the White Sox before an announced crowd of 33,333 at Comiskey Park. No doubt the red-hot Cubs were the big draw that night. The downtrodden White Sox were drawing their biggest crowds in the handful of home games they played at Milwaukee County Stadium as ownership seemed to be testing the neighboring city as a possible moving destination. That became moot the following season when Milwaukee businessman Bud Selig bought and moved the Pilots from Seattle to Milwaukee and renamed them the Brewers. Playing in the exhibition games didn't seem to be a big deal with the players. Hartig said Banks enjoyed the Boys Benefit Game because he had friends on the White Sox that he otherwise would not have gotten to see during the season.

Though Cubs fans were despondent over the late-season collapse, they made the turnstiles click 1,674,993 times in 1969 and 1,642,705 times in 1970. The team enjoyed winning seasons from 1967 to 1972. The term "lovable losers" may have been born in 1969, but the emphasis always has been on the "lovable" part because the 1969 club ended up with a winning record despite losing out on a postseason berth. As it turned out, 1969 was a way station and not a destination. And it's one fans of a certain age have wanted to visit over and over again.

On top of that, the Cubs had a good number of unsung heroes and interesting stories in 1969 in addition to their future Hall of Famers. To wit: journeyman Willie Smith (nicknamed

"Wonderful)" set the tone for the season on Opening Day, when he hit a walk-off home run against the Phillies. The clip continues to be played in Chicago to this day. Smith was an outfielder, but he gained some acclaim as being a pitcher/out-fielder early in his career. He is the only Black player in major league history to appear in at least 20 games as a pitcher and 20 as a fielder.

Another clutch performer was "Gentleman" Jim Hickman, who played from 1962 to 1966 on woeful Mets teams and then joined the Cubs in 1968 after spending 1967 with the Los Angeles Dodgers. Quiet by nature, the then-32-year-old Hickman became a cult hero with the 1969 Cubs with his penchant for hitting walk-off homers. One can still hear Brickhouse bellowing, "Hickman did it again!"

Selma, another former Met, came to the Cubs in late April of 1969 in a trade with the San Diego Padres. When the Cubs were building their lead, Selma would grab a towel in the left-field bullpen and lead the Bleacher Bums in cheers. Alas, things when south for Selma in September, when an errant pickoff throw to third base in Philadelphia led to another September defeat.

Pitcher Bill Hands, nicknamed "Froggy" by his teammates, was a solid starting pitcher. He finished the season with a record of 20–14 and an ERA 2.49.

Catcher Bill Heath was behind the plate for most of Holtzman's no-hitter. However, he was hit by a foul ball off the bat of Bob Didier in the eighth inning and suffered a broken hand. Hundley was in the hospital with a severe ear infection and missed the game. After Heath went out of the game, he was replaced by Gene Oliver. Heath never played another big league game.

And for Santo the 1969 season instilled in him a lifelong hatred for Shea Stadium, where he suffered the indignity of having his hairpiece singed by heating coils above his head in the radio booth during the opening series of the 2003 season.

Those and so many other stories were why people loved and continue to love the 1969 Chicago Cubs. "People related to the Cubs," Williams said. "You had people lined up after games waiting for autographs."

That never ended. "Another reason why that team is so popular is that so many of them played together for such a long time—of course that four of them were Hall of Famers certainly doesn't hurt," Hartig said. "Actually, growing up, I never thought of them as the '69 Cubs. They were simply the Cubs of my youth. They were the reason why I became a Cubs fan. They were there in 1970, 1971, 1972, and later. Ernie became a coach and later worked in the front office. Randy and Billy also served in coach roles. Fergie was back in the 1980s and later coached. Ronnie joined the radio booth. And all of them were regulars at the Cubs convention, telling stories and signing autographs."

Of course, Cubs fans wanted the team to win in 1969 for Mr. Cub. Banks was 38 years old in 1969 but still productive with 23 home runs and 106 RBIs. He was an All-Star for the 14th and final time of his career in 1969. For most of his Hall of Fame career, Banks played for Cubs teams that were hopelessly out of the pennant race before the ivy bloomed at Wrigley Field. The 1969 season was Banks' best chance to make it to the postseason for the first time in his career. It also turned out to be his last, as the Cubs fell short again in 1970 and 1971, his final year in the big leagues. In *Let's Play Two*, Rapoport writes of Banks driving home from Wrigley Field after the Cubs were eliminated from the pennant race. "Banks stopped his car along Lake Michigan wept," Rapoport wrote. He quoted Banks as saying, "I thought it was in the bag, but the bag broke."

It was that kind of story that made 1969 so poignant and so bittersweet for Cubs fans. But bitter they weren't, instead emphasizing the sweet parts of the 1969 season. The Cubs owned the town in 1969. The White Sox were in the midst of one of the darkest periods in team history. The Bears went 1–13. The Blackhawks failed to make the playoffs in the spring of 1969. And the Bulls, an expansion NBA team in 1966, were still trying to gain a foothold in the city.

Former Bleacher Bum Murphy says you had to "be there" to fully appreciate the 1969 Cubs and all they meant to their fans. "The 1969 Cubs team is beloved by Cubs fans, who were born prior to 1961. The first thing we must do is agree on what age most lifelong baseball fans first fell in love with the game before we can answer this seemingly innocuous question," he said of why the 1969 Cubs remain so beloved. "Me? I fell in love with the game of baseball and the Cubs in 1958. I was seven years old. The Cubs had an exciting, fun year with five of their players hitting 20-plus home runs—a really big deal back in those days—and the first of two consecutive MVP seasons for Cubs slugger and future Hall of Famer Ernie Banks. In 1958 I watched probably every Cubs game on TV on the weekends— and once grade school let out the first week of June, every Monday through Friday game until second grade began the day after Labor Day. Of course, we are only talking home games, as road games were never televised by Good Old Channel Nine...It was this love affair between the raucous Cubs and their raucous fans, which is why the 1969 team is still beloved—unless you were born after 1960, that is. Being born after 1960 means you can't possibly get it. You had to be there to get it. In fact, it is now often easy—and common—sport for people born after 1960 to naively say, 'Why are those loser 1969 Cubs so beloved? *They didn't win anything,*' which is a weak and ignorant take."

13

The 1997 Season

MANY PEOPLE BELIEVE THE GOLDEN ERA OF CHICAGO CUBS baseball—at least in terms of popularity as a franchise—began in 1984 when they won their division and made it to the postseason for the first time in nearly *40 years.* It was an exciting team, which included National League Cy Young winner Rick Sutcliffe and MVP Ryne Sandberg. But the seeds of the team's national popularity actually were planted a few years earlier. Two events helped that along. By the late '70s, their games were being broadcast across the country on WGN. Anyone in the nation could potentially watch the Cubs—something that was new to sports at the time. The franchise picked up fans everywhere. The second event turned into an even bigger moment in Cubs history: the team hired popular broadcaster Harry Caray. He would become a beloved icon of the North Side in Chicago. The combination of those three things: a fun 1984 season, games on national TV, and Caray vaulted the Cubs into another stratosphere of attention.

But as it turns out, they still weren't winning very much. The two playoff years in the '80s—1984 and 1989—came and went without any sustainability. Caray turned out to be more popular than the players in many of the years in between a rare winning season. By the 1990s the Cubs were drawing millions of fans and a large audience on their superstation, but they were still known as the "lovable losers." No modern-era season would exemplify that more than 1997.

The Cubs began that year losing their first 14 games, a National League record that stands to this day. As bad as they were, they only came two-thirds of the way to the Major League Baseball record for losses to start a season. The 1988 Baltimore Orioles began the year 0–21, a mark many think will never be broken. That same season, the Atlanta Braves began the year 0–10, which was the previous National League record for most consecutive losses to begin a year. The Cubs blew by that mark and tacked on some more for good measure. The 1997 team epitomized the brand of baseball the Cubs had built for generations. They were really bad.

Perhaps the signs were there well before the Cubs played their first game in 1997. The previous year the team finished the season with a 76–86 record but lost 14 of their last 16 games in 1996. So add that to the first 14 of 1997, and the Cubs actually were 2–28 over the course of the ending of one season to the start of the next.

And it's not like the team went on a huge free-agent spending spree or initiated headline-making trades that offseason. General manager Ed Lynch did sign pitchers Mel Rojas and Kevin Tapani, but Rojas wouldn't even last the season. He was traded to the New York Mets, while Tapani began the year injured. It led catcher Scott Servais to utter these less-than-hopeful thoughts during the spring: "The chance of us getting into the playoffs without Kevin Tapani is not realistic," Servais said in March of 1997. "Few teams have deep enough pitching to survive the loss of a guy like that. I know we don't."

That idea would prove to be extremely prophetic in the weeks to come as manager Jim Riggleman took his club to Florida to start the season against the Marlins, which would begin a murderers' row of opponents.

Game One—April 1, Pro Player Stadium
Marlins 4, Cubs 2

No one could know at that moment the Marlins would go on to win the World Series in 1997, but the mismatch on the mound on Opening Day told its own story. Florida starter Kevin Brown was at the top of his game, coming off a season in which he compiled a 1.89 ERA.

Meanwhile, Cubs starter Terry Mulholland was in the middle of a solid career but at age 34 wasn't exactly the ace the opposition employed. He produced a 4.66 ERA in 1996, giving the Marlins the pitching edge. It would be a major the theme over those first few weeks. "We knew going in who we were facing our first 10 games or so," Riggleman said. "It was the Marlins and Braves and then the Marlins again. They had Kevin Brown and Alex Fernandez and Al Leiter. And then of course you had the Braves staff, right? Those first couple of weeks we knew we were overmatched."

The Cubs managed one hit over the first eight innings of Game One, trailing from the second inning on.

Game Two—April 2, Pro Player Stadium
Marlins 4, Cubs 3

Much like the first game, the Cubs trailed early and managed little offense, finishing with just five hits on the day. Starter Steve Trachsel gave up all the runs in what would be the first of four, one-run losses during the streak. Leiter got the win for the Marlins.

The Cubs rookie left fielder that day, Doug Glanville, went 1-for-4 in the loss. "I remember facing Leiter in Florida and getting a hit and I was in the euphoria of being a young player to some degree at that moment," he said. "I had a certain cluelessness around. After a while I realized the reason we were losing so much was because we were playing against these great pitchers. I mean, who faces all these guys in the first two weeks? We did."

Game Three—April 3, Pro Player Stadium
Marlins 8, Cubs 2

This would be the loss, which would essentially snowball into the rest of the streak. Cubs starter Frank Castillo gave up five runs in the first inning, sinking any hope of salvaging a game in the series. But most important was star first baseman Mark Grace injuring his hamstring. He wouldn't play again until losses No. 13 and 14. "Grace never got hurt, but he pulled something, and that really impacted our offense," Riggleman said. "He was right in the middle of everything we did. Sammy [Sosa] wasn't himself to start the season either, but losing Grace was really bad."

What was already a bad start to the season was exasperated by a misunderstanding on the team's charter flight out of Florida. "I think the airline was like Miami Air or some charter flight like that, and [infielder] Rey Sanchez tried to order a drink, and there was a dispute on how Rey did it," Glanville said. "The flight attendant just wasn't happy with how it came across. And so that was really between Rey and her, but then Sammy comes in behind that and orders a drink, and she said something like, 'Ask me nicely.' And Sammy didn't know what was going on, and she said it again, 'Ask me nicely,' and so it turned into this whole thing, and the traveling secretary had to come over and separate everyone. Nerves were getting rattled. Maybe none of that happens if we win a game. You're just in a better mood when you win."

Game Four—April 4, Turner Field
Braves 5, Cubs 4

The Cubs keep up a trend of trailing early in games while giving up 15 hits on the day, while earning only seven of their own. Grace missed his first full game while middle-of-the order players Sandberg and Sosa struggled. Sosa's batting average dropped to .071 after four games. And this came after Sosa just had a torrid spring—at least for most of it. "I remember making a joke that Sammy might go 30/30 at spring training," Lynch said. "But then he was kind of going through the motions toward the end, and I know Jim talked to him near Opening Day."

Said Riggleman: "He's such a violent swinger, and so we shut him down for a few days because he had a slight tweak in his back. But then I was kind of pushing him back on the field a little bit. It was like, 'Hey, we're going to be facing Glavine, Smoltz, Fernandez, Kevin Brown, Leiter, maybe you should do more than the batting practice pitching that you're facing out here right now.' So we got him back on the field for probably the last game or two of spring training, but he wasn't the same guy who was hitting a homer every other day. That carried over."

Game Five—April 5, Turner Field
Braves 11 Cubs 5

Just like in Florida—after playing a close game the night before, the wheels came off the next day. The Cubs actually took a 3–2 lead as they scored off of John Smoltz. That was an accomplishment in itself. Things were finally looking up—until a five-run fifth inning turned Game No. 5 into yet another loss. Finishing the affair the next day due to weather delays didn't change the outcome. "Already, we were feeling the effects of losing Kevin Tapani to that finger injury," Lynch said. "Everyone had to move up a spot. That was such a killer to miss him while we were playing the best teams in the league."

Tapani had just signed a three-year, $11 million deal with Chicago after going 13–10 and pitching 225 innings the previous season with the Chicago White Sox. He was a key offseason addition for the Cubs who simply wasn't available until later in the season. "We were counting on him as our No. 1 or No. 2 starter, and he's not pitching for us," Riggleman said. "So he's shut down. He was supposed to pitch the first game of spring training, and the pitching coach tells me about this finger issue."

Tapani had surgery in late March on his index finger. He didn't appear in his first game as a Cub until June. It was bad luck for him and the Cubs, which would follow them throughout the streak.

Game Six—April 6, Turner Field
Braves 4, Cubs 0

Of course it would be Greg Maddux to deliver the first shutout of the season as he threw eight shutout innings *against* his former team. On top of having little offense, the Cubs made four errors, easily leading to loss No. 6. So Brown, Maddux, Smoltz, Leiter, and Fernandez all had beaten the Cubs over the first week of the season. They were feeling overmatched. "We just faced a historically talented group of pitchers all in a row," Glanville said. "I faced Brown that series against Florida before, or maybe it was another one, as a pinch-hitter. And up until that day, I had never seen a sinker like that. I remember swinging over the first two pitches, and they ended up like almost hitting the plate. And I remember stepping out like, *What in the world was that?* So the last pitch, he threw another sinker, and I don't think I've ever did this since, but I took a swing with my knee on the ground. I got so low to make sure I hit it and I pounded it into the ground to short and I was literally celebrating that I made contact."

Weak contact was about the best the Cubs could muster against that group of pitchers. A combination of Grace's injury and slow starts to the season by hitters—against top pitching—doomed their opening week. It would continue in that manner as the team began round two against Florida and Atlanta—this time at home.

Game Seven—April 8, Wrigley Field
Marlins 5, Cubs 3

The home opener would draw 35, 393 fans, but they would not go home happy as a day off and a return to Wrigley Field did little for their favorite team on the field. Sosa did hit his first home run of the season but was still batting .160 by day's end. Without Grace in the lineup, Sosa's lack of production was a killer. But in baseball you can't make fun of a struggling player as much as an injured one. "By now, we're teasing Grace because we're losing, and he's not in there," shortstop Shawon Dunston said. "We're like, 'Gracy, man, you're the best hitter on the team and you don't want to play against the best pitchers.' I said, 'I know you're hurt, but c'mon.' He got mad a couple times, but we knew he wanted to play. We were getting killed out there."

Glanville added: "I know when you're hurt and can't help the team you feel invisible. I know that's how [Tapani] felt. I'm sure Mark, too."

Game Eight—April 10, Wrigley Field
Marlins 1, Cubs 0

The Cubs offense sunk to a new low as they were one-hit by Fernandez, who pitched a complete game while striking out eight without issuing a walk. He nearly no-hit the Cubs, but

Dave Hansen singled in the ninth to stave off further embarrassment. By day's end, not one of the eight starting position players for the home team was hitting even close to .200. Batting averages ranged from shortstop Dunston's .074 to outfielder Brant Brown's .185. It was as dismal at the plate as anyone could imagine. "Yeah, I can't remember who had the highest average, but I knew it wasn't me," Dunston said with a laugh. "I remember looking at the box score, and one guy was at .200, and everyone else was at like .100. Ooh, that was bad. We needed a break from those All-Star pitchers, I guess."

Game Nine—April 12, Wrigley Field
Braves 2, Cubs 1

The Cubs third, one-run loss in four games came in the ninth inning when Jeff Blauser drove home the go-ahead run off Rojas, the Cubs' closer. Even though the game was played on a Saturday, the Cubs drew only 23, 944 fans. No one wanted to watch an anemic offense. They would draw even fewer over the final three games of their homestand, but that didn't faze the players. Back then, it really took a lot to upset a Cubs fan. "Man, they are the best," Dunston said. "I mean, they were okay with us, but it was pretty tough. It was very embarrassing when you're a professional, and you're 0–10 or whatever we were, and the whole team is hitting under .200. It wasn't just me; it was the whole team. There was just not even one guy having a good year."

Game 10—April 13, Wrigley Field
Braves 6, Cubs 4

The Cubs offense woke up a little against Tom Glavine, but it wasn't enough to stave off loss No. 10 in a row. That tied the record—ironically set by the Atlanta Braves in 1988—for most consecutive losses by a National League team to begin a season.

It's not a record anyone wanted to be associated with. "At that point, somebody asked from the front office, 'Hey, Jim, what's going on? Why can't you win a game?'" Riggleman said. "And I told them in a nutshell: 'We've played 10 games, we've got 50 hits, the opposition has a 100.' That wasn't an exaggeration. That was a fact. We were at getting out hit two to one. That's how you lose 10 in a row."

The exact numbers were 104:54. The Cubs had given up 50 more hits than they earned over the first 10 games of the season. It was an outstanding ratio in such a short period of time. It was hard to know what was worse: their offense or pitching.

Game 11—April 15, Wrigley Field
Rockies, 10 Cubs 7

The Cubs were starting to feel better about themselves at the plate, but now their starting staff was consistently putting them in a hole. Kevin Foster lasted just three innings in loss No. 11 and saw his ERA over the first few games balloon to 8.00. The Cubs hit three home runs that day from Brooks Kieschnick, Dunston, and Brian McRae. All hit their first of the year, but the team was no closer to a win.

It was at around this time that Riggleman had some harsh words for his team: "Yeah, those games against Colorado gave me the opportunity to get on the ballclub a little bit," he said. "'Hey guys, this is embarrassing. That was bullshit.' I wasn't going to address it when we were playing those other teams because they just outplayed us. [Florida and Atlanta] were two of the best teams in the game. We played hard. We just couldn't hit their pitching, and they could hit ours. But now we got sloppy."

Dunston's memory coincides with that of Riggleman, who he called "Rags." "Rags was very professional. He wasn't yelling or screaming. Our effort was good for those tough opponents,"

Dunston said. "He got on us a little when it waned. We did have the right manager because Riggs was very calm. He wasn't those old-schools guy like Earl Weaver. If Earl Weaver was involved, we would have been in real trouble. Things would have fallen apart."

Game 12—April 16, Wrigley Field
Rockies 4, Cubs 0

The appearance of the Cubs offense over the previous few days was short-lived as it was shut out for the second time in the first 12 games to a pitching staff, which would finish with the highest ERA in the NL that season. Roger Bailey—not exactly a household name—did the honors that day, going the distance in front of just 13,890 fans. It would be the smallest home crowd of the season. Once again, tensions were high as the team embarked on its second road trip of the season without a win. "I remember two rookies, Kevin Orie and Ramon Tatis, getting into a fight over a seat on the bus," Glanville said. "Somehow it turned into a shoving match, and people were taking swings. And I remember Brian McRae was like, 'If they're going to kill each other over a seat, just let the rookies fight.' Nobody was interested in stopping it. I don't know if that happens if we win a few games."

At least Grace would be ready to return to the lineup for the next series. All he could do over the past 10 days was watch as the team sunk to new lows. "We're 0–12 for a reason," he said. "We've played lousy baseball."

Game 13—April 19, Shea Stadium
Mets 6, Cubs 3

Bad weather in New York postponed Game One of a series with the New York Mets, giving the Cubs two off days before their next game. It didn't matter, as once again the winless visitors got behind in the game in the very first inning. It would mark the eighth time in 13 games the Cubs would give up first-inning runs as they dropped to 0–13. "I remember talking to some guys that I knew that were involved with the '88 Orioles, when they get off to that 0–21 start," Lynch said. "And they said, 'Hey, the only thing you can do is just try to protect. Deflect as much negative attention away from the organization and keep it on yourself. You have to keep it away from the players.' And so I took as much responsibility as I could. I'm the one that put this team together, and if anybody's to blame, it's me."

Game 14—April 20, Shea Stadium
Mets 8, Cubs 2

Game One of a doubleheader against the Mets would prove to be the last of the consecutive losses as once again an opposing pitcher went the distance against the Cubs. Bobby Jones gave up five hits and a walk over nine innings while Grace homered for the Cubs. It was Grace's second game back from his hamstring injury, nearly coinciding with the end of the two-week nightmare for the organization. "I didn't know that would be our last loss, of course," Dunston said. "But I'm pretty sure I was thinking, *We can't lose both games of the doubleheader*."

Game 15—April 20, Shea Stadium
Cubs 4, Mets 3

A win! *Finally*. The Cubs earned their first victory of 1997 in the nightcap of the doubleheader against the Mets. Of course, it wasn't easy. They led 4–1 going into the bottom of the ninth. "Rojas was our closer," Riggleman said. "And we need to win a game so bad. I got him in there with one out in the eighth. He gets out of the eighth, but he comes limping off the mound. He pulled something. Can you believe this? So now we're going to have to start somebody else for the ninth."

So after waiting all that time to use his newly-signed closer, Riggleman had to turn to righty Turk Wendell to finish off their first win. A single, strikeout, wild pitch, and a walk later, the Mets had the tying run at the plate in Todd Hundley. There's one out. Wendell got him swinging. "We finally got away from playing Florida and Atlanta," Glanville said. "We had a shot at a win!"

But it would have to wait one more batter as Lance Johnson—a name that would be important to the Cubs later in the season—doubled home two runs, cutting the lead down to just one. But Manny Alexander, also a name to remember, grounded out to short to end the game, and the Cubs had their win, though if the game had been played about a decade later, it may never have happened. "They hit a ground ball to [Jose] Hernandez at short," Riggleman said. "He throws a one hopper over to Grace. Grace makes one of his tremendous picks out of the dirt, just tremendous, but he cheated like crazy coming off the base. If there was replay, he would've probably been called safe, but Grace sold it. And that's how we got our first win."

The celebration was a little bit more than a usual late April victory. "Yeah, we had a nice time," Dunston said. "I mean, we really did enjoy it more than a normal win. We were off the schneid. Now we're going to go on our own streak."

The Cubs did beat the Mets 6–4 the next day but lost their next three games. A long winning streak was far from their minds. Things would get better—after that three-game skid they won four of five—but losing the first 14 games of the season buried the 1997 Cubs in the standings. But out of failure sometimes comes a glimmer of hope. That moment occurred midseason, when Lynch made a big trade with the team they had beaten months earlier to break the skid in the first place. "I remember it very well," Lynch said. "We made a deal with the Mets. Our scouts really liked pitcher Mark Clark a lot. Lance Johnson had a lot of ability. We like him. Manny Alexander was the same way. And we just thought, *Let's just try to inject some new blood into this team.*"

On August 8, 1997, the Cubs traded Rojas, Wendell, and McRae for Johnson, Alexander, and Clark. It changed the dynamic on the team and set them up for something no one saw coming: a playoff berth the very next season. "This is an important part of the story," Riggleman said. "Mark Clark was 6–1 for us after the trade. [Tapani] comes back after that operation and he goes 9–3. So as the manager, I look back. We were 15–4 with those two guys in the second half. Now we have a kid coming up next year named Kerry Wood, and Lance Johnson and Mark Clark were solid players. We became way more respectable."

THE STREAK BY THE NUMBERS

0 wins
14 losses
Opponent runs scored: 78
Cubs runs scored: 36
Cubs final record: 68–94, last place in the NL Central

PART 5

THE ODDITIES

14

Shining Light on a Myth

MARK TWAIN SAID, "THERE ARE THREE KINDS OF LIES: LIES, damned lies, and statistics."

This is a story about a damned lie, a damned lie that's taken on a life of its own for almost 40 years. Now let's get one thing straight: Folklore, mythology, and legend are all parts of what makes following sports so much fun.

Did Babe Ruth really call his shot in the 1932 World Series against the Chicago Cubs at Wrigley Field? Probably not, but we'll never know. And whether he did or not doesn't really matter. He still homered off Charlie Root, and the New York Yankees went on to win the game and the World Series. Could Negro Leagues legend Cool Papa Bell really turn out the lights and be in bed and under the covers before the room got dark?

Highly unlikely, but it's a fun piece of baseball lore. Those bits of baseball bombast not only are fun, but they're also perfectly harmless.

There is one episode in Cubs history that is out and out hokum. It is flat-out inaccurate. It is utter misinformation. And it's disrespectful to history. In other words, it's a damned lie. And it's time the record be set straight once and for all. What we're talking about here is the false notion—spread by some of the principals involved and believed by many to this day—that the Cubs lost the home-field advantage to the San Diego Padres in the 1984 National League Championship Series because Wrigley Field did not have lights.

Nothing could be further from the truth.

Here is the bottom line, and then we will start from the beginning and find out how a damned lie was born and took on a life of its own: the 1984 NLCS proceeded as originally scheduled with the Cubs (the National League East winners) playing and winning the first two games of the best-of-five series before the Padres won the next three games all in San Diego.

There is a situation where the Cubs would have lost home-field advantage because of the lack of lights at Wrigley Field. That would have been in the World Series against the Detroit Tigers. That stubborn fact—as John Adams might have called it—has been lost to time. Just why is somewhat mystifying since we're talking about something that happened in 1984, not 1884.

But nevertheless, this lie has persisted.

It's not entirely accurate to say the Cubs were eternal hold-outs against night baseball at Wrigley Field. The first night game in major league history was played on May 24, 1935, at Cincinnati's Crosley Field. Night baseball, which already had been played extensively in the minor leagues and Negro Leagues, was seen as a way to increase attendance and enable working people to get out to ballgames during the depths of the Great Depression. Other teams began taking note of what the Reds had done, and one by one, they installed lights in their ballparks. The Brooklyn Dodgers were second, and on June 15, 1938, the Cincinnati Reds' Johnny Vander Meer made history by tossing his second consecutive no-hitter in that game.

In Chicago, the White Sox, still reeling from the Black Sox scandal of 1919, installed lights at Comiskey Park in 1939, and on August 14, 30,000 fans came out to see the Sox beat the St. Louis Browns 5–2. The entire season home attendance for the White Sox that season was 594,104, up from the 338,278 they drew in 1938 (when the Cubs won the National League pennant, drawing 951,640 fans to Wrigley Field).

Where it gets interesting for the Cubs is that they were prepared to install lights at Wrigley Field for the 1942 season. But after the December 7, 1941, attack by Japan against the United States at Pearl Harbor, prompting U.S. entry into World War II, Cubs owner P.K. Wrigley instead donated the materials for the lights to the government for the war effort.

After the war Wrigley was no longer interested in illuminating his ballpark at night, preferring to sell day baseball at "beautiful Wrigley Field." It remained that way through the Cubs' lean postwar years, when they finished well out of the running for the next two decades.

The Cubs finally awoke from their on-field doldrums in 1967 and held first place for a brief time and in 1969 they looked a surefire bet to win the new National League East as they ran out to a nine-game lead on August 16. But a late-season collapse by the Cubs coupled with a charge by the upstart New York Mets ended the North Siders' postseason hopes.

If the Cubs had made the postseason in 1969, the issue of lights or no lights at Wrigley Field would not have been a factor.

Baseball in those days was still hidebound by tradition, and all postseason games were played during the day. It wasn't until 1971 that the first night World Series game was played, but the trend toward prime time was inexorable. More and more night games were introduced in the World Series, and the last day game in the Fall Classic was Game Six of the 1987 World Series at Minnesota between the Twins and the St. Louis Cardinals.

In 1984 the Cubs became a sensation. The Tribune Company bought the team from the Wrigley family in 1981 and soon thereafter brought Dallas Green in from the Philadelphia Phillies to run the baseball operations. Green, a big and brash former pitcher, managed the Phillies to a World Series title in 1980. He set about changing things in Chicago by "Building a New Tradition" at Wrigley Field. Along those lines, one of Green's early proclamations was that the old ballpark eventually would need lights for the Cubs to be competitive. Green also knew there were some players who could not burn the candle at both ends, playing day baseball and enjoying Chicago's night-life at the same time. The "or else" part of the lights equation was that if the ballpark didn't get lights, the Cubs might have to find a new home in the Chicago area. No direct threat was made, but the seed was planted.

Green modernized the entire operation and set about not only building a new tradition, but also rebuilding a moribund Cubs farm system. Under Green's watch the Cubs eventually produced players such as Joe Girardi, Jamie Moyer, Rafael Palmeiro, Mark Grace, Shawon Dunston, and a pitcher named Greg Maddux.

The first couple of years under Green's stewardship were rough. The Cubs finished 1982 with a record of 73–89 and 1983 at 71–91. Manager Lee Elia, Green's handpicked choice, vented his frustrations with the losing in a memorable and profane tirade (preserved on tape by late Chicago radio maven Les Grobstein) on April 29, 1983. Elia's mistake was tearing into the fans, saying that 85 percent of the world is working, and that the rest were coming out to day baseball at Wrigley Field. You never, ever attack the paying customer, but Elia somehow kept his job, at least temporarily.

Green's "new tradition" was looking like more of the same old, same old as 1984 dawned under new manager Jim Frey. During one stretch of spring training, the Cubs lost 11 in a row, and their Cactus League record stood at 3–18. On March 26, as spring training was winding down, Green obtained outfielders Gary Matthews and Bob Dernier from the Phillies in a trade for Bill Campbell and Mike Diaz. It wasn't the first time Green fleeced the Phillies. After the 1981 season, he stole a young infielder named Ryne Sandberg and veteran shortstop Larry Bowa from his former club in a trade for Ivan DeJesus. The Cubs won four of their final six games in spring training to finish the 1984 Cactus League season at 7–20.

The spring 1984 trade changed the Cubs. Matthews provided leadership and offense, and Dernier teamed with Sandberg at the top of the order to form "The Daily Double," as announcer Harry Caray dubbed it. The Cubs held their own on a season-opening road trip, going 3–4 in games at San Francisco, San Diego, and Los Angeles. They finished April with a 12–8 record. They didn't have a losing month all season, hanging close to first place all summer.

On June 13 Green pulled off a major deal, obtaining pitcher Rick Sutcliffe (who later would become a chief spreader of the NLCS myth) from the Cleveland Indians in exchange for Mel Hall and Joe Carter. Sutcliffe and the Cubs both caught fire. He went 16–1 with the Cubs on the way to the National League Cy Young award.

Just 10 days after the trade, a season-defining game took place at Wrigley Field. Known as "the Sandberg game," the Cubs rallied from a 7–1 deficit against the St. Louis Cardinals to win 12–11 in 11 innings. Sandberg hit a pair of game-tying homers—one in the ninth inning and one in the 10th against relief ace and former Cubs pitcher and future Hall of Famer Bruce Sutter. The crowd of 38,079 went delirious, and the game was televised nationally on NBC, when the *Game of the Week* was still a big deal.

As the summer wore on and the Cubs showed they were for real, Wrigley Field was the place to be. The bleachers became fashionable. Once the cheapest seats in the house, they became the place to be seen (many of the fans were derided as "yuppies" who weren't interested in the game), planting the seed with management to transform the bleachers into some of the highest priced tickets in the ballpark in subsequent years. The Cubs wound up drawing 2,107,655 fans to Wrigley Field, marking the first time in their history they had drawn at least 2 million at home.

By August it was clear the Cubs were serious playoff contenders. They were the perfect Cinderella story—the team that hadn't been to the postseason since the 1945 World Series. The Cubs were ready for prime time. The trouble was their ballpark wasn't because it lacked lights. And many people wanted for that never to happen. In August of 1983, the Chicago City Council passed an ordinance by vote of 42–2 to prohibit the playing of night games at Wrigley Field. There was opposition to lights from many residents in the neighborhood, some of whom operated under the acronym CUBS (Citizens United for Baseball in Sunshine).

Major League Baseball had TV networks ABC and NBC to please. NBC had the rights to the World Series. With a huge investment at stake, the network wanted as many prime-time games as possible. That could not happen at Wrigley Field if the Cubs were going to make it to the Fall Classic. There was talk of playing Cubs home games in the World Series at either Comiskey Park or Milwaukee County Stadium should the team make it that far. There was also short-lived talk of installing temporary lights at Wrigley Field, something that the city likely would have rejected, per the ordinance.

In those days home-field advantage for both the American and National League Championship Series and the World Series alternated year by year without regard to teams' records. The 1984 National League Championship Series was scheduled for two games at the home of the NL East winner followed by three games (if necessary) at the home of the NL West winner. In 1983 the opposite arrangement was in effect. The 1984 World Series was scheduled to begin with two games in the National League park, followed by three games at the American League park, followed by the final two (if necessary) at the NL park.

The issue of no lights at Wrigley Field presented a huge problem to Major League Baseball and their TV partners. What would be done to satisfy all the interested parties? In late August, Jerome Holtzman, the "Dean" of Chicago baseball writers and someone well sourced within MLB management circles, accurately reported in the *Chicago Tribune* how Major League Baseball commissioner Bowie Kuhn would rule: the NLCS would go on as scheduled, but in the event the Cubs won and advanced to the World Series, the first two games would be at the AL team's park, followed by three at Wrigley Field, followed by two (if necessary) back at the AL park. Holtzman wrote: "Here is a double prediction: The Cubs will wind up with a split: No lights at Wrigley Field for the playoffs or Series, a victory for the Cubs; the Series will open in the American

League park, a loss for the Cubs because it would deprive them of their home-field advantage. Assuming the Cubs win the National League pennant and assuming also the Series goes the seven-game limit, the middle three games would be played in Chicago, not the last two."

That was the only change. Games One, Two, Six, and Seven of the World Series would be played in prime time on weeknights in the American League City. Games Three, Four, and Five would be played over the weekend during daytime hours at Wrigley Field.

Nothing changed as far as the NLCS was concerned. Here is how respected baseball writer Thomas Boswell sized it up in his column for *The Washington Post*: "Bowie Kuhn passed his gut check yesterday. No lights in Wrigley Field. No change in the National League playoff schedule. No Chicago Cubs postseason 'home' games played in other teams' parks. No goofball warping of the World Series schedule. No kowtowing to the preferences of network TV. No fear of the anger of baseball's owners who will lose millions of dollars in TV revenue because of Kuhn's decision."

So there it was: "No change in the National League playoff schedule." Can we say it again louder for those in the back? *No change in the National League playoff schedule.*

When it was all said and done, though, the entire point became moot. The Cubs won the first two games of the NLCS at Wrigley, and Sutcliffe even hit a home run in Game One. Cubs fans and some in the media were counting their chickens, which never would hatch. The Padres swept the final three games of the series at Jack Murphy Stadium, and the Cubs were left heartbroken again. The World Series between the Padres and the Detroit Tigers reverted to its original format, and the Tigers won in five games on their home field, Tiger Stadium.

Cubs fans, who were hoping of a sort of rematch of the 1945 Series between the Cubs and Tigers (arguably a better matchup than Padres–Tigers ended up being), were left to dream of what might have been. The Cubs lost. Their fans were heartbroken. But nobody was cheated.

There was always "next year," as there invariably was with the Cubs. The talk in early 1985 was that new MLB commissioner Peter Ueberroth would consider moving Cubs postseason games, even to (egad!) St. Louis. That position intensified in March 1985, when Circuit Court Judge Richard Curry ruled to uphold prohibitions against night games at Wrigley Field. Somewhat whimsically, Curry wrote: "[O]ne 'Homer in the Gloamin" [Gabby Hartnett's twilight homer in 1938] is worth a hundred hit into the blackness of night," and "future generations should not be deprived of seeing the shadows creep across the infield."

The Cubs were favored to repeat in the NL Central in 1985 and got off to a good start. But injuries to the pitching staff destroyed the team's chances. On June 11 the Cubs were in first place with a four-game lead. But they proceeded to lose 13 in a row and finished the once-promising season with a record of 77–84 and in fourth place. The Cubs had losing seasons in 1986 and 1987, when Green resigned over philosophical differences with Tribune Co. higher-ups, who felt they no longer had to endure Green's bluster.

The Cubs didn't make it back to the postseason until 1989 (thanks in large part to players Green had drafted and developed), and by that time, Wrigley Field had lights, which were installed in time for the first game to be played on August 8, 1988. The 8/8/88 game got underway, but a rainstorm (divine intervention perhaps) washed the game out before it could become official, and the first night game didn't take place until the next day.

That should have been the end of the story when it came to the 1984 Cubs. But it wasn't. Somewhere along the line, and it didn't take long, a narrative was created that the Cubs somehow got cheated out of home-field advantage in the NLCS because Wrigley Field didn't have lights. That false narrative was spread from all manner of outlets—local and national—and from Cubs participants, who should have known better.

In a timeline story about the installation of lights at Wrigley Field, *Chicago Sun-Times* writer Bill Braden wrote on August 8, 1988: "Having won their division, the Cubs open the National League playoffs against the San Diego Padres in the first of two home day games at Wrigley Field. They win both games, then fly to San Diego—where they lose three games and the playoffs. If they had had lights, they could have played three home games instead of two."

From the *Chicago Tribune* in July 1992: "And, lest we forget, that was the year they stole a home playoff game from the Cubs. "The Padres weren't responsible. The commissioner of baseball was. But the Padres cashed in when the commissioner said the Cubs had to forfeit home-field advantage because Wrigley Field lacked lights at the time and three day playoff games would hurt television revenue. You remember what happened. The Cubs, who were entitled to three home games, swept the only two the commissioner let them play at Wrigley. Then they lost three straight in that colossal concrete hot tub they call Jack Murphy Stadium to choke the five-game series. As a result, a city full of fans, who only show up at games when it's fireworks night or white zinfandel night or no-sulfates night—those fans went to the World Series, while long-suffering Cubs loyalists went home."

It's one thing for TV talking heads to get this wrong, and many did over the years, but it's quite another for a newspaper reporter—with archives at his or her disposal—to do so. That didn't stop others. Writing in the *Chicago Sun-Times* in August 2003, Carol Slezak weighed in, incorrectly: "The Cubs already had been burned by not having lights. In 1984, they were forced to give up home-field advantage in their playoff series against the Padres. After winning the first two games of the series, day games at Wrigley, the Cubs played the next three games in San Diego and lost all three. If only for one more home game…"

The story went on to quote Sandberg. "When it's a best-of-five playoff series and you have a home game taken away, that plays a very big role," he told the paper. "For postseason games, for the World Series, for All-Star Games, it was important to get lights."

It was just as bad on the national stage. Author Rich Cohen wrote this in the August 2001 issue of *Harper's Magazine*: "In 1984 the commissioner of baseball was more concerned with the fact that no night games at Wrigley meant the league would be robbed of prime-time TV revenue. As a result, the Cubs, in a great miscarriage of justice, were stripped of their home-field advantage, which, in the best-of-five playoff, proved crucial."

The only miscarriage of justice here was that done to the truth. One local scribe who got it right was *Chicago Sun-Times* columnist Ron Rapoport, who authored *Let's Play Two*, the 2019 biography of Ernie Banks. On May 21, 1986, less than two years after the 1984 NLCS, Rapoport wrote, using a healthy dose of sarcasm: "The lack of lights at Wrigley Field already has cost the Cubs a berth in the World Series, said the million-dollar anchor man who frowns a lot. The Padres were given an extra game in San Diego for the 1984 National League playoffs. Right, responded the million-dollar anchor man whose head bobs up and down a lot. Of such poor memories is hysteria bred. The Cubs would have lost a game at home had they made it to the Series, but their failure to get that far took place in complete accordance with the rules. Revisionist history, however, is not the enemy here. Believing the evidence of our ears is the real problem."

Media members getting things wrong is one thing even if they have access to accurate archival information. Those who took part in the games should know better. Outfielder Jay Johnstone, a colorful member of the 1984 Cubs, said this to *Chicago Tribune* columnist Steve Rosenbloom in 2005: "Everybody talked about the goat [curse] in Wrigley Field, and remember because we didn't have lights in the 1984 playoffs, the San Diego Padres were awarded the final three games because the commissioner's office wanted to have night games."

Frey, who managed the Cubs in '84, had this to say to the *Tribune's* David Haugh in 2005: "We [didn't get] our home-field advantage. You can't deny the effect the home field had."

Haugh corrected the record in the next paragraph of the column.

Even former front-office executive Green got into the revisionist history game. Speaking to the *Tribune's* Paul Sullivan in 1998, Green took credit for the lights debate but got his facts wrong. Sullivan, who knows Chicago sports history as well if not better than any journalist, added the brackets to clarify. "I started the lights controversy," Green told Sullivan. "And I was the one who met with all the neighborhood people. We won [the National League East] in '84 and [would have] lost home-field advantage [in the World Series]. As a result of not having lights, that really got the ball rolling—then the threat of the league moving [home playoff games] to a neutral site."

In subsequent years to 1984, Green somewhat ironically admitted to understanding the appeal of day games at Wrigley

Field. "Day baseball attracts fans," he told Sullivan in the 1998 article. "I've turned [180 degrees] on it. I don't think the *Tribune* or anyone in Chicago should push for all night baseball. I was a night baseball person when I came on because I was born and raised on night baseball. When I got there, it took me a while to understand and appreciate the day baseball thing. It's a tremendous thing for families, for young people, for people we haven't been able to attract to games."

Whether it has been in the broadcast booth or during public appearances, Sutcliffe also has played his part in perpetuating the myth of the Cubs losing home-field advantage in the 1984 playoffs. Al Yellon, a longtime season-ticket holder in the bleachers, authors the Bleed Cubbie Blue blog. He laid the brunt of the blame for this myth at Sutcliffe's feet. "[H]e'll tell you that the Cubs were at a disadvantage because Major League Baseball took away a home date from the Cubs in the National League Championship Series, forcing them to play three games in San Diego," Yellon wrote in 2018. "Usually, Rick's listeners nod knowingly and repeat this story to the point where it's become an article of faith among some Cubs fans. 'MLB stole our home field!' people have said and continue to say. 'And that's why the Cubs lost!' They didn't, and it wasn't."

So how did we get to this point? To the point where so many people believe fake news that's simply not true despite mountains of evidence to the contrary? Yellon theorized that Sutcliffe "has conflated the fact that the Cubs would have lost home field in the World Series had they made it with the fact that they never were supposed to have home field in the NLCS anyway but wound up losing the series. It makes a better story to tell that the Cubs had something taken away and maybe that's why they lost, even if it isn't true, which it wasn't and isn't."

Perhaps it was an early case of gaslighting. Or maybe it's nothing simpler than saying something over and over again, and people will believe it, whether it's true or not. "Chip Caray [former Cubs TV announcer] and Dallas Green repeated over and over again the story that the Cubs would lose a home game," said research historian Ed Hartig. "But, no, the truth was the alignment was every other year East vs. West, and this was the year National League West was going to have home-field advantage. Now, they would have lost a home game in the World Series. It was supposed to be National League for two, American League for three, National League for two. Because of the [lack of] lights, they would have put it on the weekend [at Wrigley Field]. So, yes, they would have lost a game there. But sometimes it's more important to tell the story than to tell the truth. Then people hear that story, and they pass it on because they got it from Sutcliffe or they got it from Dallas Green. And after awhile, you tell it enough times, and it becomes the truth."

Another reason may be changes in the makeup and number of media members covering sports nowadays. "It goes back to the changes in the beat," surmised Mark Ruda, who covered the Cubs for the *Daily Herald* in 1984 before moving to the White Sox beat, where he covered the South Siders' 1993 division championship. "When I first started covering baseball in '84, it was basically us beat writers and TV along for the ride at the end. Flash forward to '93 when I was covering the Sox. You had this thing coming up called sports talk radio. If you were covering baseball back in '84 on a big metro paper, you were the final arbiter of truth, along with your copy desk. If a mistake was printed and promulgated and not corrected, it became truth. How many times have we seen even now where a lie becomes truth and reality? The point I'm trying to get to is there's less of a chance of that happening today—believe it or not with as bad a shape as the media is in—because in '93 we had competition with sports talk radio. And after I left [the beat], there was this thing that was going to go nowhere called the Internet with all these websites and whatever. There's probably everybody in press boxes from blogs and websites and whatever. There's a lot more people to keep you honest. I think there's less of a chance of that happening now because it's not just one or two gatekeepers of truth in Chicago anyway. In New York there's more, even back then. L.A., too. I think the democratization of media—for all its faults and a lot of it being total bullshit, too, with an ax to grind—I think that's part of it, too. Myth becomes reality after awhile in American society."

Since the installation of lights, night games have become a way of life at Wrigley Field. At first, the Cubs were allowed to play 18 home night games at home. That has increased gradually over the years to the point where the Cubs play about half their home games under the lights, and big-name concerts account for other nighttime usage of the ballpark. Friday night games are generally prohibited during the regular season, but the Cubs have gotten a couple exceptions, and postseason games can be played on any night at Wrigley. The Cubs have won a National League pennant under the lights at Wrigley Field and they've played three World Series night games at home.

Night games no longer are a big deal at Clark and Addison, and if current Cubs management and ownership had their druthers, they'd likely have the Cubs play the majority of home games at night, making them like every other club in the big leagues. For current Cubs fans, the fight over lights at Wrigley Field is ancient history. That's the kind of stuff that breeds myth. Hopefully this clears up the myth of 1984 once and for all. But let's not count on it. Sometimes truth is poorly lit.

15

Pranks

PRANKS ARE A TIME-HONORED TRADITION IN BASEBALL, AND the Chicago Cubs employed many players over the years who were willing and able to pull one over on their teammates. Everyone has seen the bubble gum bubble on top of the baseball cap of an unsuspecting player, while he sits in the dugout oblivious to everyone staring and laughing at him. That prank is as old as baseball itself. Leaners are another popular prank often used when teams take to the road. That entails leaning a bucket of water up against the hotel door of a player—only to see it spill inward as he opens it. Whoever knocks on the door would be far from the scene by the time the player answered it. At that point, he wouldn't know who to blame until someone admitted to the hijinks. Then there's the more dangerous ones, which sometimes include lighting something on fire—be it shoelaces, baseball caps, or something even more valuable. Can a prank be taken too far? Of course, but the good ones know where to draw the line. The Cubs had a lot of good pranksters pulling off both simple and complex pranks.

Ryan Dempster

Ryan Dempster played 16 years in the big leagues for five different teams, but the bulk of his career was spent with the Chicago Cubs. He was known for having a good sense of humor and for keeping things light around the clubhouse. His Harry Caray impression always brought laughs—and so did his pranks. "The best one was the Will one, right?" Dempster asked rhetorically.

Will Ohman, a left-handed reliever, pitched for the Cubs over five seasons from 2000 to 2007. He was Dempster's teammate for his final three years with the team. "I never planned on really pranking him," Dempster explained. "It started because somebody did the frozen shirt trick and the frozen shoes to him."

A teammate had frozen Ohman's shirt and shoes and put them back in his locker. Dempster claims it wasn't him. "He was hellbent on finding out who did it and kept bugging Tim Busse, our strength coach, about it over and over and over," Dempster said. "And finally, I just told Busse, 'Tell him it was me.' I kind of wanted to see what Will would do."

Dempster pitched in a spring game that day, meaning his locker area was unattended while he was on the field. "When I got back, my entire wardrobe was messed up," Dempster said. "My shoes were retied, eye black in the rim of my hat, zipper glued shut. I proceeded to get rocked in the spring training game."

Ohman had done a similar trick in the minors to a teammate, messing with his clothes, but he had a rule not to cause damage to something that would need replacing. He figured he and Dempster were even. "I thought it was over," Ohman said. "Boy, was I wrong."

Dempster sought some big-time revenge. After all, he says he didn't do the initial prank on Ohman in the first place. But the youthful reliever had gotten Dempster back anyway. Said Ohman: "I was too young and stupid to even fathom something as extravagant as what he was planning."

Dempster put his plan in action the following day. "I had two friends from MLB productions in town and I told them to come to the field the next day—and bring a camera," Dempster explained. "So we proceeded to take Will's car during batting practice, jack it up on some blocks, take the four tires off, and hide them around the stadium."

Talk about an elaborate plan. This prank needed access to Ohman's car and time to take off the tires. Former Cubs pitcher Glendon Rusch was in on the joke, too. "I'll never forget seeing his face when he walked down to the bullpen, and one of the wheels of his car was down there," Rusch said with a laugh. "There was one in the shower. Watching his face was priceless."

Ohman didn't think twice of the tire he saw in the dugout when he came out for the day's game, but when he walked down to the bullpen, things began to click. "We get down there, and someone from the elevated bullpen said to me, 'Hey, is this your wheel out here?'" Ohman said with a laugh. "That's a question you don't expect when you get down to the pen. I proceed to search the field for my tires over the next two-to-three innings."

Ohman found one in the shower, one in the dugout, one in the bullpen, and one in the coach's office. "It was just a sinking feeling," Ohman said. "He's just going to make this miserable. I figured if I counteract, he's going to burn down my house."

But there *was* more. Dempster wasn't done with Ohman. "At the same time—and this is the best part of the prank—Will thought they were doing like a *30 for 30* [documentary] on left-handed relievers," Dempster said. "Remember, MLB productions was there. They were following him around, and he was just strutting around like a peacock, thinking they were doing this big special on him. But it was all about his car, which was really great. Oh my God, that was a really good prank!"

No one was immune to Dempster's trickery. Current clubhouse attendant, Danny Mueller, was a victim back when he was a batboy for the team in 2009. "This was a hard one but really worth it in the end," Dempster said. "We told him that he was doing such a good job as a batboy that he actually got voted to the All-Star team for that job. We had a press release made up and everything."

Eventually, the other clubbies had to break it to him that batboys don't get voted into the All-Star Game, but Mueller and his family got to attend the game anyway. "That was like one of those ones where it had to have a happy ending because that would've been heartbreaking otherwise," Dempster said. "He couldn't believe that we would actually do that to him. I got him and his family some tickets to go the All-Star Game. So that was definitely a good one that ended well."

Dempster just couldn't sit still. There were times when he would join the ground crew or dress up as different mascots throughout his career, including Gapper, the Cincinnati Reds' canine mascot. "Oh yeah," Dempster said. "I did that for like six innings. I got on top of the dugout and everything. And for anyone that thinks that's easy, it's not. I ran over like six kids and almost threw up in that costume."

Being the culprit of so many pranks made Dempster a target as well. There were plenty of teammates who wanted to get back at him, including fellow pitcher Ted Lilly. Like many tricks pulled on teammates over the years, this one happened in spring training. It's a good time of year for pranks, considering the outcome of games were meaningless, and players had extra time on their hands. "So we were having like a friendly competition of doing some fun stuff to each other in the dugout like with cups of water and stuff," Dempster said, "like you pour water down the back of a guy's sock, and we'd do it throughout the game. Just easy stuff like that."

The next day was scheduled to be a short one for Dempster and Lilly. Neither was pitching, which means they were allowed to leave for the day after five innings of that day's spring game were complete. "We were going to Talking Stick Casino," Dempster said. "We wanted to get out of there fast."

Dempster jumped in his rented car and started toward the casino, getting on the highway which heads north toward Scottsdale, Arizona. "After about five minutes of driving," Dempster said, "I get a text message from Lilly that says, 'Don't rub it.' That's all it says. I have no idea what that means."

About five minutes later, Dempster would fully understand what it means. "I started to feel this kind of intense burn in my groin area and I'm like, *Oh my God, this dude put red hot in my underwear*," Dempster said. "So now I'm on the 101 highway, and it's rush hour traffic. I'm not going anywhere quick, but it's burning. So now I proceed to drop my drawers down and take my underwear off as I'm driving. And then I get rid of my underwear and I put my pants back on and then I realized Ted's a smart pranker because…he put it in my jeans as well."

Dempster arrived at the casino and met his teammates at the blackjack table while feeling, well, not himself. "So I never responded to the text, and now they're all looking at me, and I wasn't going to let them know how much pain I was in," Dempster said. "I'm like sweating. I'm uncomfortable. And I just sit down and I'm like, *Nope, not going to let him know*. And he's just looking at me. He's like, 'You don't feel anything?' Finally, I'm like, 'You son-of-a bitch. You totally got me.' That was definitely a good one. I can appreciate it even if it was done to me."

Rick Sutcliffe

There may not be a player in baseball history who has more stories—and had more fun—than the great Rick Sutcliffe. He was acquired mid-season in 1984 and would play for the Chicago Cubs until 1991. Sutcliffe won the Cy Young Award that first year in Chicago after going 16–1. He finished second for that same honor in 1987, assuring himself as one of the team's best pitchers of that era. He was also one of their best jokesters.

One of his favorite pranks occurred in 1988—courtesy of then rookie first baseman Mark Grace. He was also a gregarious player, but rookies are supposed to be seen and not heard—and are easy targets. "I was starting that day and I had been told that we were going to get rained out," Sutcliffe said. "Of course, the day I pitch, I had my Walkman on, and everybody knew not to talk to me. I didn't talk to anyone. I didn't even talk to my wife the day I pitched."

It's a tradition that stands to this day: most starting pitchers want to be left alone the day they are scheduled to start. That could include family, friends, and, of course, reporters. In fact, media members are told not to approach a starting pitcher in the clubhouse on the day he's pitching unless they're interested in getting yelled at. Sutcliffe was no different but took the superstition to an extreme as he was even unwelcoming of teammates. "So Mark Grace looks at the chalkboard in the clubhouse, and it had him hitting seventh that day," Sutcliffe said. "So him and I and whoever was hitting eighth, we're hitting in the same group."

Sutcliffe was referring to batting practice before the game. Players are grouped together and told a certain time they'll hit on the field or in the indoor cage. In this case the bottom three hitters in the lineup were in the same hitting group. "Well, because its bad weather, we're hitting inside," Sutcliffe said. "Gracie didn't know where the batting cages were, so he comes up and he taps me on the shoulder, and I'm sitting in my locker with my music on, and I look up and I don't even take my headphones off. I'm like, *What? What, what the f--- do you want?* And he tapped me again, and I said, 'What?' And he goes, 'It says, 'hitting in the cages.' I noticed we're in the same group. I don't know where the cages are.'

"Well, while he's saying this, my mind starts racing," Sutcliffe said. "Instead of sending him to the cages out underneath the bleachers in right-center, I sent him out in the concourse, where there's 30,000 people trying to get out of the rain."

Before Wrigley Field underwent renovations, players would have to cross the outfield and enter a door under the bleachers in order to get some swings in. When the weather was poor, it was the only indoor cage. Nowadays, both the Cubs and the visiting teams have indoor cages near their clubhouses. "Instead I send him all the way from our clubhouse to the visiting Cardinals clubhouse," Sutcliffe said with a laugh. "He's got his bat, he's got his helmet on, he's got spikes on, and he's out there and he's gone for like 30 minutes. I told him, 'When you think you've gone too far, keep going.'"

Grace followed the concourse around from the third-base side, where the Cubs clubhouse was, to the first-base side, where Sutcliffe sent him. "Sure enough, he gets there, he walks in, he turns the corner, he goes up the stairs, and he's staring head on at [Cardinals coach] Red Schoendienst, one of his heroes," Sutcliffe said. "Gracie grew up a Cardinals fan. And he looked at Red and he goes, 'Hey, you guys must still be hitting now. When do we hit?' And Red goes, 'I don't know who the f— you are and I don't know why you're here, but you're in the Cardinals clubhouse and you need to leave.'"

Grace finally returned to the Cubs side, where Sutcliffe was howling when he heard the whole story. "My favorite part is he had to come all the way back through those fans, and a lot of them were asking him, 'Why are you in the Cardinals clubhouse? Grace, what's wrong with you?'"

"Finally, he makes it back and is like, 'Okay, you got me good.' Then he goes, 'Now, really, Sut? Where are the cages?'"

No one was immune to Sutcliffe's antics. Even the batboy got taken by the Cubs right-hander. When a game was dragging, according to Sutcliffe, play-by-play man Harry Caray would ask the television producer to get word to Sutcliffe that the broadcast needed some "energy." The veteran pitcher was more than happy to oblige. "They would call down and ask, 'Is there anything you could do?'" Sutcliffe said. "I go, 'Yeah, just watch the batboy. I'm going to send him to the home-plate umpire, asking for the keys to the batter's box.'"

Of course, there are no keys to the batter's box. Sutcliffe was sending the batboy on a wild-goose chase. "It was all set up ahead of time," Sutcliffe said. "Right before the end of an inning, I would ask for the keys, and someone would yell out that the home-plate umpire had them. So I would call the kid over and tell him when the inning was over to go ask the umpire for the keys to the batter's box."

The umpires were in on the prank. So when the batboy ran out to home plate, they were ready to play their part. "The kid would go to the home-plate umpire first," Sutcliffe said. "He'd pat his pockets looking for it, then send him out to the second-base umpire. Same thing. Then he would go to first base."

Meanwhile, television cameras were capturing the whole thing. Finally, the first-base umpire would put his arm around the batboy and say, "Young man, do you play baseball?"

"Yes, sir."

"Um, do you know what the batter's box is?"

"Yes, sir."

"You know that there's no keys to the box."

When the inning break ended, Caray would play the whole exchange for the television audience. "I know Harry loved that one," Sutcliffe said. "And the ballboys all laughed and got a tape of it afterward. To this day, I hear from them."

Sutcliffe met many famous people during his time as a major league pitcher. They became subjects of his pranks as well. No one was safe. "I used to leave tickets all the time for celebrities," Sutcliffe said. "There was one time that [comedian] Tom Dreesen asked me to leave tickets for David Letterman. I did this to the actor, Mark Harmon, as well. I would put their seats right behind one of the big concrete poles [with] the obstructed view."

Wrigley Field has several seats under that obstructed view designation. People in those seats would have to peer around a pole, which helped keep the stadium upright. It's far from the best seat in the house. In fact, you can't see the field without straining your neck. "I would have them sit there like right up until the first pitch and then I would have the usher go get them and bring them down to the good seats," Sutcliffe said. "It was always fun to look up in there and just see them looking out, kind of leaning one way and the other, trying to figure out how to look. That was a fun one."

It might come as a surprise to see Hall of Fame second baseman Ryne Sandberg in this section. Known as mild mannered and even quiet by fans and members of the media, Sandberg was anything but to his teammates. In fact, that laid-back reputation may have aided him when it came to pranks. So just imagine Sutcliffe and Sandberg teaming up on a prey—except Sutcliffe wanted nothing to do with this next prank. In this one instance, he claims he was an innocent bystander—at least for a moment. "Ryno was the big hot foot guy," Sutcliffe said. "He used to light everybody up—and then blame me."

The hot foot prank is pretty simple but can be difficult to pull off. The prankster's goal is to light the shoe laces or even just the shoes of his potential victim on fire. The key is getting to a player's feet while he's being distracted by the game or something else going on in the dugout.

On this particular day, Sandberg's victim was a teammate who played just one season with him and Sutcliffe: Terry Francona. The eventual longtime manager played first base and outfield for the Cubs in 1986. "So he gets Francona with the hot foot, and I think Chris Speier as well, over the course of a week," Sutcliffe said. "And [Sandberg] blames me. And they believed him!"

So Sutcliffe was on alert for retaliation. He knew Francona or Speier was coming for him, but Speier actually wasn't sure who pulled the latest hot foot on him so he warned Sutcliffe. "Chris comes over right before the game and he's sitting by me and he's all nervous and he's like stuttering," Sutcliffe said. "And he's looking off, and I go, 'Spy, what the heck are you doing?' And he goes, 'Sut, don't, please, please don't beat me up.' He says, 'Tito is sliding underneath the bench. There's an opening underneath there and, and he is going to light you up.' They put rubbing alcohol on my shoelaces so that they'd just blow up when a match was lit. Once you put a match to it, it would just blow up. Can you believe these guys?"

Francona was now underneath the bench, literally getting ready to light his teammate on fire. Sutcliffe plays it off for as long as he can. "Tito is sliding underneath there, and we just kept talking, and I could hear: all of a sudden, the big lighter goes off," Sutcliffe said. "And I jump up, and Tito's laying underneath there looking at me, and I suddenly throw the cup of Gatorade I'm holding on him. Then I take the lid off the big Gatorade cooler, and as he's trying to crawl back out, I throw *that* on him. I'm just crushing him with ice and everything I could find."

At this point, Francona is soaked. He's not in the starting lineup so there's plenty of time for him to go back up to the clubhouse to change. Or is there? "Our manager, John Vukovich, loved this," Sutcliffe said. "So we're in the bottom of the first, and Tito's in the shower, and Vuk is yelling for him: 'What the f--- are you doing? You're pinch-hitting. So-and-so got hurt. You're in the on-deck circle.' Tito comes running out. He has spikes on with no socks. He has pants on with no belt. He has a shirt. He comes running, no batting gloves, nothing. He comes running out, grabs his bat, and I mean, everybody started just roaring at Tito. Now that was a good one."

Francona couldn't deny he was often the object of Sutcliffe's attacks. In fact, that wasn't the only time Francona had to change jerseys due to Gatorade being dumped on him. "That f------ guy," Francona said. "He would give me a cup of red Gatorade. I thought he was a nice guy, but there would be a hole in it. So I would get it all over my uniform…We were bad, but we had fun."

Sandberg was an unsuspecting villain, a "quiet assassin," according to Greg Maddux. "Back then we didn't have all the TV and the video games and the iPhones and iPads," Sandberg said. "We had to make up our own entertainment in the locker room, whether it's three hours, four hours before a game, or whatever it might be. And we had rain delays as well. So there was some time for fun."

Sandberg played for the Cubs from 1982 to 1994 and again from 1996 to 1997 so he had years to perfect his craft. In fact, he was notorious for pulling pranks. He focused on one particular teammate. "One of my favorite teammates that I could think of was Gary Matthews, the Sarge," Sandberg said. "He was a character and he was a little bit of a style master but also a good aggressive baseball player. He took things seriously, which made it even more fun."

Sandberg and Matthews were teammates for only three-and-a-half seasons, but Sandberg made the most of it. Matthews was an intense but fun-loving player. When it was time to play, he put his game face on. Other times, well, Sandberg got to him. "I got a kick out of doing a little trick on him every now and then," Sandberg said. "At Wrigley Field we used to have director's chairs in front of our lockers. Those are the soft, canvas ones. What I had learned was the part about the seat. If you took out the two wooden dowels that go in there—that holds the canvas seat in place—if you kind of took those out and just put the canvas back without those in there, the person would sit down and go all the way to the ground."

Sandberg waited for the perfect time to terrorize Matthews— usually when he came into the clubhouse feeling good about himself or the team before a game. "If you can picture Sarge coming in and talking trash a little bit about the game and who's pitching that day, he'd be saying something like, 'We're gonna beat up on that guy' or 'We're gonna kick some butt' and just using his positive influence that he had four hours before a game. He's holding a cup of coffee, too," Sandberg said with a laugh. "Now I watch him as he approaches his chair and I've rigged that canvas [seat]. And I kind of go to the other end of the locker room pretending to talk to somebody, and he sits down on his chair and goes all the way to the floor with a cup of coffee, which goes everywhere. It was hilarious."

Would Matthews get upset? "Ryno was like an irritating nephew," Matthews said. "He got me a few times with those kinds of pranks."

Sandberg added: "He was lighthearted as far as that goes. He kind of acted like the tough guy, but I know that he got a kick out of it. I did it to him a couple of times. It was great."

Maddux, the Hallot Fame pitcher, swears he didn't participate in a lot of pranks, but he loved seeing others pull them off. Like many, he witnessed Sandberg torture Matthews. "I saw him put ammonia in the bathroom around the toilet," Maddux said. "And then he lit it on fire, where [Matthews] was sitting there in the morning, [doing his business]. And all of a sudden, he's got a fire going on around him that lasted for about 10 seconds."

Matthews actually thought that prank went a little far. He could have been hurt. "They rigged it so I could only use one stall," he said. "He had poured alcohol everywhere. The whole bathroom was on fire. I came out and told him he was lucky I liked him so much."

Said Maddux: "He was just sitting there yelling and screaming at Ryno. That was probably the best one I saw."

Sandberg had become a star in 1984, helping the Cubs to the division title. It gave him leeway in the clubhouse that perhaps others didn't get. "Of course, with him being the MVP, any pranks that he did that year was kind of all bets off," Matthews said.

One of the rules of playing in the big leagues was dressing professionally on road trips. Players would wear suits to the airport and on planes and then to the team hotel. Matthews was a snappy dresser, and Sandberg knew it. "This is when I was smoking cigarettes, and Ryno had the reputation of putting those little pellets in your cigarette. So when you light it, it blows up," Matthews said. "And the cigarette would get all over your nice suit. He would do that repeatedly. It's one of the reasons I actually stopped smoking."

Kyle Schwarber

The Chicago Cubs' fourth pick in the draft in 2014 was a fun-loving outfielder from Cincinnati who had a Midwest sense of humor. It included some self-deprecation—especially about his defense. Schwarber was a converted catcher, playing left field for his tenure with the Cubs from 2015 to 2020. He got better over time but had some moments he'd like to forget, especially when teammate Jon Lester was on the mound. Schwarber simple seemed to commit a lot of mistakes when Lester was pitching.

Lester is known as one of the Cubs best free-agent signings of all time. He was a leader in the clubhouse and finished his career with exactly 200 wins. Like Schwarber, Lester helped the Cubs break a 108-year championship drought before leaving the team after the 2020 season.

To honor such a great player, Schwarber and his teammates decided to make a video for Lester as he began his good-byes to Chicago just after the regular season ended in 2020. "It was a video of me just messing up a bunch of plays in left field while he's pitching," Schwarber said, laughing. "And then in between, they had me talking about what a pleasure it was to play for Jon when he was on the mound."

As Cubs players began a workout on the field one afternoon, they made sure Lester's attention was on the video scoreboard. "We sat him down like it was going to be like this big emotional video," Schwarber said with a smile. "It was all Rizzo's idea.

He's like we have to do this and have you talking about what a pleasure it was to play behind him."

Sarah McLachlan's "I Will Remember You" played underneath the montage, which included moments of Lester getting angry. But the final sequence showed Schwarber tracking down a fly ball in slow motion and making the catch as Lester pumped his fist into his glove in approval. "Yeah, that was fun," Schwarber said. "I caught one in the end for him."

Tommy La Stella

A 25th man on the roster type of player for the Chicago Cubs, Tommy La Stella excelled as a pinch-hitter during his four years with the team from 2015 to 2018. Eventually, he would become a starter in the league, but whether you're a starter or bench player, no one parks in the boss' space.

In spring of 2018, La Stella parked his rental car in then-general manager Jed Hoyer's parking spot in front of the Cubs practice facility in Mesa, Arizona. That turned out to be a mistake—but also the start of a fun prank war. "I parked in Jed's spot, and in retaliation he took my uniform from my locker and replaced it with khakis," La Stella said. "I had to practice in them. So next time, I had a kid's bounce house set up in his and Theo Epstein's parking spots."

The kid's bounce house took up several parking spots, leaving Hoyer and President Epstein to park elsewhere when they arrived. At least some players' kids had some fun that day though. The front office would eventually get the last word on that prank.

During the next home spring game, the front office sent a message back to La Stella courtesy of the video scoreboard at Sloan Park, the team's spring stadium. A first message read: "TOMMY, NOD THAT IT'S OVER"

Then the next one really ended it for La Stella: "TRUCE?"

"THANK YOU, TOMMY."

"GOOD LUCK IN LOVE...AND IN IOWA."

Iowa, of course, is where the team's Triple A affiliate is located. It was a not-so-subtle message that if the prank war didn't end, La Stella was on a one-way trip to the minors. Of course, Hoyer and Epstein were kidding, but the message was received. "Then I knew it was over," La Stella said with a laugh. "No prank is worth a trip to the minors."

Acknowledgments

I OFFER PROFUSE THANKS TO RESEARCH HISTORIAN ED HARTIG for his comprehensive knowledge of Chicago Cubs history and his willingness to be a second pair of eyes. Mark Ruda not only was generous with his time in talking about Sammy Sosa's days with the Chicago White Sox, but he also literally showed me the clubhouse door when I began my baseball writing journey with the *Daily Herald* back in 1989. Twenty-two years on the Cubs beat were made easier by my predecessor, Barry Rozner. A media member always appreciates the cooperation of the team's media relations staff. My early days on the Cubs beat were made more enjoyable by Sharon Pannozzo and Chuck Wasserstrom, both of whom gave generously of their time for this book. In the later years on the beat, Peter Chase and Jason Carr helped to make comprehensive coverage possible. Also with the Cubs, Jim Oboikowitch put me in touch with Joanne Biebrach, granddaughter of Gabby Hartnett for the chapter on Gabby's homer in 1938. Thanks to Joanne for her graciousness. Much appreciation to former Cubs manager Jim Riggleman and to former Cubs general manager Jim Hendry for their candor.

You don't survive on the baseball beat without sharing a few laughs, along with plane rides, drinks, and meals with your newspaper teammates and friendly competitors from other papers and outlets. Those colleagues include Paul Sullivan, Mike Kiley, Jeff Vorva, Teddy Greenstein, Carrie Muskat, Jordan Bastian, Mark Gonzales, Gordon Wittenmyer, Toni Ginnetti, Mike Imrem, Rozner, Scot Gregor, the late Bill Jauss, Kelly Crull, Patrick Mooney, Sahadev Sharma, coauthor Jesse Rogers, and others too numerous to mention. My apologies for not naming everyone. A tip of the cap to Al Yellon of Bleed Cubbie Blue for pointing me to electronic newspaper archives. That streamlined the research immensely.

Cubs radio announcer Pat Hughes is a storehouse of information, and his partner, Ron Coomer, provided me with a player's perspective.

No one completes a project like this without the full support of family members. Thanks to Arlene, Liz, Steve, and Sarah for putting up with my baseball geekery for these many years.

—B.M.

It was wonderful to catch up with Cubs players from my youth, including those quoted in the book like Greg Maddux, Andre Dawson, Ryne Sandberg, Rick Sutcliffe, and Gary Matthews. Countless others gave me good ideas or just allowed me to reminisce with them. I'm very much appreciative of their time.

—J.R.

Sources

Books

Helyar, John. *Lords of the Realm.* Villard Books, 1994.

Lowry, Philip J. *Green Cathedrals.* Addison-Wesley Publishing Co., Inc., 1992.

Owens, John, and David J. Fletcher. *Chili Dog MVP.* Eckhartz Press, 2021.

Rapoport, Ron. *Let's Play Two.* Hachette Books, 2019.

Sandberg, Ryne, and Barry Rozner. *Second to Home.* Bonus Books, Inc., 1995.

Newspapers/Magazines

Chicago Sun-Times

Chicago Tribune

Daily Herald

Daily Southtown

The Washington Post

Sports Illustrated

Websites

Mlb.com

Sabr.org
Baseball-Reference.com
Fangraphs.com
Bleedcubbieblue.com
Nbcsports.com/Chicago

About the Authors

Bruce Miles has chronicled the Chicago sports scene since 1979. He covered Major League Baseball for 31 years, including 22 as the beat writer covering the Chicago Cubs for the *Daily Herald*. He and his family live in the northwest suburbs of Chicago.

Jesse Rogers has worked in Chicago media for more than 20 years, including 10 at ESPN, where he covered hockey and baseball. His favorite moments include reporting on the 2010 Chicago Blackhawks' championship as well as the 2016 Chicago Cubs' World Series win. He's also the coauthor of *Try Not To Suck*, the book on former Cubs manager Joe Maddon.